ELISABETH'S JOURNEY 1945

*To Mary —
With Best Wishes,
Love, Renate*

RENATE SHAVE

January 2011

© Renate Shave, 2009
Elisabeth's Journey

ISBN 978-0-9561281-0-2

Published by
HILLSIDE PUBLICATIONS
128 Alinora Crescent
Goring-by-Sea
West Sussex BN12 4HJ

The right of Renate Shave to be identified as the author of this work has been asserted by her in accordance with the Copyright, Designs and Patents Act 1988.

All rights reserved. No part of this publication may be produced in any form or by any means – graphic, electronic or mechanical including photocopying, recording, taping or information storage and retrieval systems – without the prior permission, in writing, of the publisher.

A CIP catalogue record of this book
can be obtained from the British Library.

Book designed by Michael Walsh at
THE BETTER BOOK COMPANY

Cover design by Ian Tyrrell

Printed by
ASHFORD COLOUR PRESS
Unit 600 Fareham Reach
Fareham Road
Gosport
Hants PO13 0FW

DEDICATION

I dedicate this book to my late husband,

Geoff Shave, who died in St. Barnabas Hospice,

Worthing, West Sussex

I would like all proceeds from the sale of this

book to go towards the new building

of this Hospice.

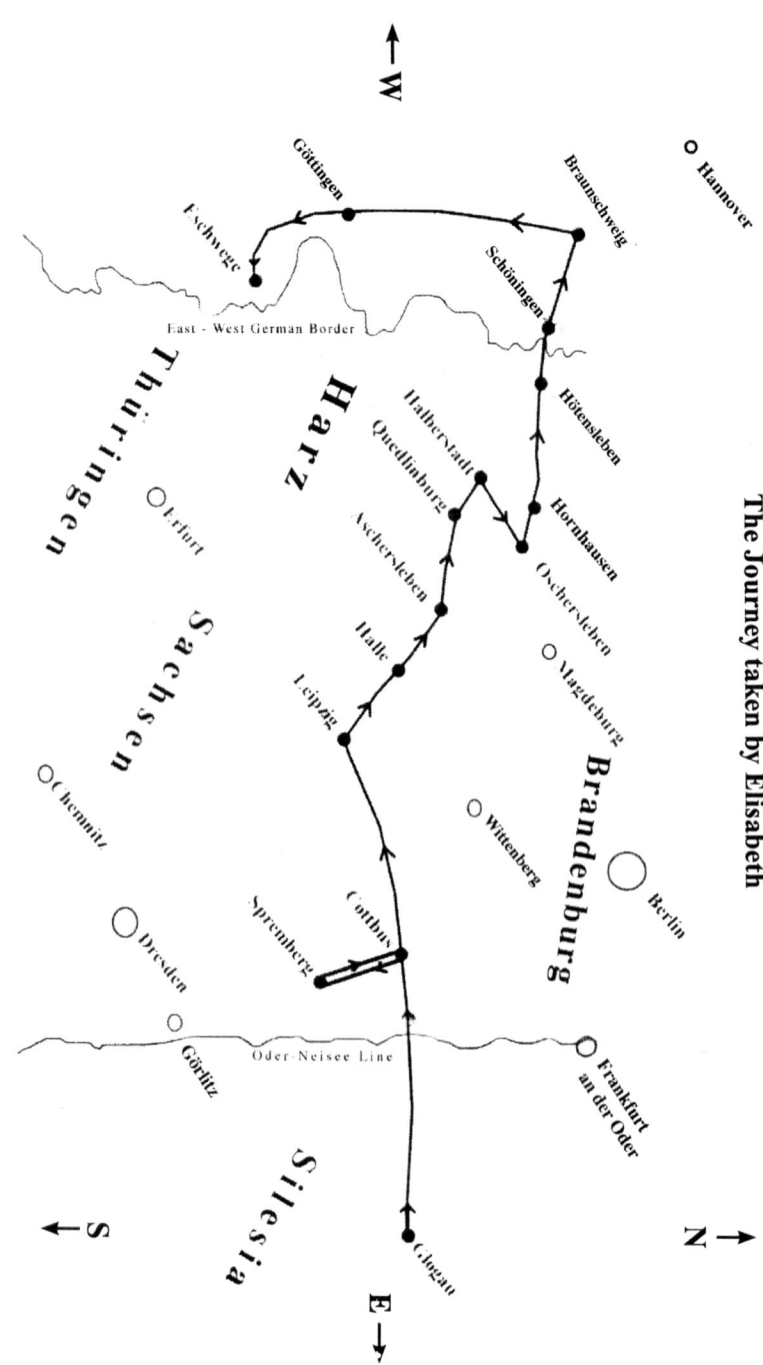

DEDICATION

I dedicate this book to my late husband,

Geoff Shave, who died in St. Barnabas Hospice,

Worthing, West Sussex

I would like all proceeds from the sale of this

book to go towards the new building

of this Hospice.

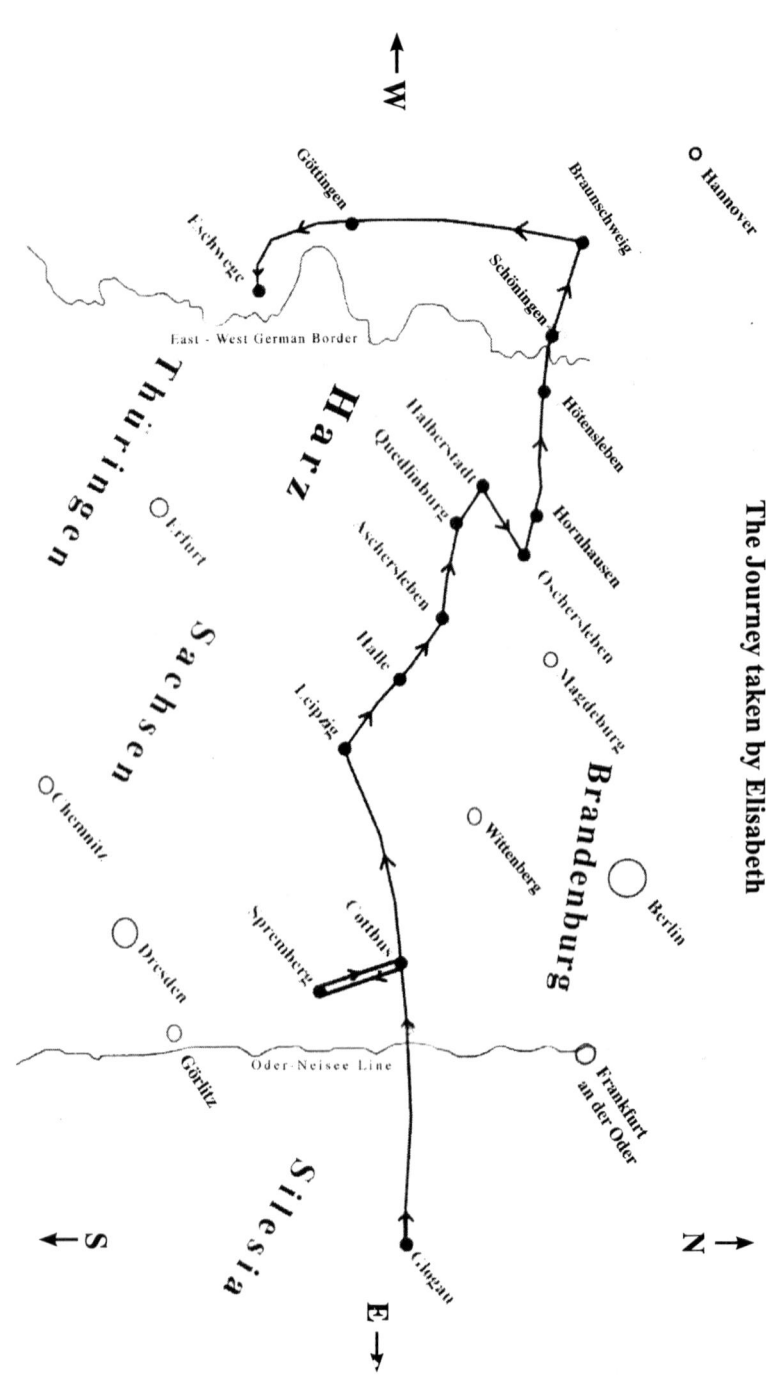

CONTENTS

    Acknowledgements i
    Prologue iii
1   A Shocking Announcement 1
2   Preparing to Leave 5
3   Journey to Spremberg 11
4   With Frau Lehmann at Bergstrasse 8 19
5   Return Journey to Glogau 25
6   Life at Bergstrasse 8 29
7   Deciding to Leave Spremberg 36
8   On the Move again 41
9   Arrival in Quedlinburg 50
10 Move to Lindenstrasse 8 56
11 Settling In 62
12 Oma and Opa Arrive in Quedlinburg 66
13 Getting a Job 72
14 A Surprise Visit 77
15 An Air Attack – observed 83
16 Quedlinburg in Danger 90
17 The War is Over 95
18 A New Arrival 101
19 Fredo and Family come to Quedlinburg 106
20 The Russians take over in Quedlinburg 112
21 Summer Activities and a Wonderful Event . 117

22	Planning new Arrangements	123
23	Visit to Julius-Wolff-Strasse	128
24	Move to Brechtstrasse 8 – A Postcard arrives	133
25	Looking forward to the new School Year	138
26	The Second Postcard	143
27	Ludwig – Here at Last	148
28	Preparing to Leave Quedlinburg	159
29	Approaching the Border	166
30	Crossing the Border	173
31	Arriving in Eschwege	182
32	New Beginnings	194

ACKNOWLEDGEMENTS

My sincere gratitude

- to my friend Jean Ashwin and to many of my German students in Worthing, for their encouragement to tell this story,

- to my wonderful Creative Writing teacher, Jan Henley, for her expert advice and guidance throughout the writing process,

- to my fellow students at the Creative Writing Class in Southwick, West Sussex, for their continued interest and support,

- to my brother, Kurt Giertz (the Friedrich in the story) for supplying me with details of our family history, partly gleaned from a brief diary of our late father, Alfred Giertz (the Ludwig in the story).

In memory of my mother

ELISABETH

PROLOGUE

The train pulls slowly into the station
And with a long squeak draws to a halt.
Platform 3.
I look around.
Yes – here it started
Long ago
Our journey west.

Now I have come back to see my home again.
The place where I was born.
The place of happy, carefree childhood days.

I see it in a flash
Before my inner eye:
The big corner house.
A little turret high on top.
Slender windows.
Balconies with pillars.
At the side the wide entrance door.

Calming coolness envelops me on entering.
I run up two staircases
To our own apartment.
I stand on tiptoe to reach the bell.
I'm only five.
I hear my mother's footsteps
Before the door flings open.
'Hello, my darling, here you are!'

A smell of baking wafts through the narrow hall.
I turn left
Into our children's room.
I see the tall, green stove.
I lean against its shiny tiles.
So warm and smooth.
There is my cot
With all my dolls and little bear sitting inside
Waiting for me.
My desk stands under the window.
I hear children's voices from below.
I look out.
Max and Susi, Bernd and Inge
Playing in the yard.
A line of washing dangling in the breeze.
I turn back and look at Friedrich's desk.
So many books!
And there – his bed.
A little lamp beside.
He reads before he sleeps.

I step out of the station building
In bright sunlight.
Yes, I remember:
The long straight street
Stretching out before me.
I quicken my pace.
Here's the park
Where we played
Hopscotch and hide and seek.

I see the pond,
The trees,
The bushes …

A few more steps.
This is the place!

But no, it's not.

I stand – frozen.

A huge modern block of flats
Towers over me.
Yellow walls rise up.
Windows – small and square.
Balconies, squeezed in
Like matchboxes.
I count eleven storeys.
Graffiti on the lower walls.
The entrance door – grey and dull.

It opens with a jolt.
A bunch of children tumble out,
Calling to each other
In a language I cannot understand.
They draw lines on the pavement
And start their game.
They hop and shriek with laughter.
A little boy looks across
Begging me to watch them play.

v

I nod and smile.
I know what fun we had
So long ago.

I'm reconciled.

This was my home.
But now it's theirs.
Times change.
And life goes on.

                R.S. – Glogau, July 2005

1

A Shocking Announcement

It was the evening of 23 January 1945.
When the children had gone to bed, Elisabeth settled down in her comfortable armchair in the living room.

Both Friedrich and Anja had been out in the park opposite in the afternoon riding their sledges and had returned with glowing cheeks, ready for their tea. This year the snow was particularly nice and crisp, just right for sledging, and the temperature had not dropped too low. All the youngsters of the area were having a great time together.

Elisabeth was happy for her children. So far they had not suffered too much from wartime. Would they be spared the hardship so many people from further east were enduring? Her sister-in-law had passed through the town on a trek with her family and her old parents two days ago. Elisabeth had no idea where they were now.

Every day, news bulletins relayed from loudspeakers in the road brought more stories of refugees fleeing their homes.

She took out her husband's letter that had arrived this morning. Ludwig had been drafted into military service three months ago. His words were quite encouraging. He said the German army was well prepared to fight back the Russians who were approaching from the East.

Relaxing in her chair, Elisabeth looked around the room. There was the big desk where Ludwig would normally be sitting in the evenings, perhaps working on an article for the newspaper or taking a phone call from a colleague.

The grandfather clock had stopped, she noticed. She would have to wind it up tomorrow.

Only a few weeks ago a big Christmas tree had stood in the corner of this pleasant room. She couldn't help smiling when she remembered little Anja's wide eyes when she had spotted her new doll under the tree. Anja had asked Father Christmas for a doll with genuine hair and eyelids that would close and open, and it seemed a small miracle that her wish could be fulfilled at a time when everything was in short supply. One day in December, Elisabeth happened to see this beautiful doll in a shop window, with a note saying: 'Regret – no cash, exchange only. Train set wanted.' She had rushed home to explain to her son what she would like to do. Eleven--year-old Friedrich immediately agreed to sacrifice one of his two model train sets for his beloved little sister, and he had shared her delight on Christmas Eve when Anja held her 'Brigitte' tightly in her arms all evening.

What a lovely time they had all had together, singing and playing. Ludwig had been on leave over Christmas and the four of them had even been able to go to a children's theatre play, one afternoon in the New Year.

Ludwig had left on 9 January, Elisabeth's fortieth birthday.

'We'll have a big birthday party as soon as this awful war is over', he had said confidently as they all walked to the station to wave him off.

Elisabeth was just getting up to switch the radio on to enjoy a music programme, when a loud 'Achtung! Achtung!' rang in her ear from outside.

Glogau – Hohenzollernstrasse

She rushed on to the balcony to listen to the announcement which was repeated several times: 'Residents of the following roads are ordered to leave the town by tomorrow afternoon, as military defence will be put up against the approaching Russian army.'

Had she heard right? She leant over the balcony railings and listened again. Yes, her road, Hohenzollernstrasse, was among the street names given. How dreadful! So it was true what people had been talking about for some time: that their town, Glogau, would be evacuated. Secretly, she had hoped it might not happen. She stood still in the cold evening air, as the announcer went on: 'Boys from the age of eleven will stay behind and are required to report to the war office near the station building by tomorrow morning.'

Elisabeth was stunned. Her boy, to stay behind? She was beside herself with fear. How could she leave Friedrich here – a mere child, to fight the Russians?

Hastily she put on her coat and hat and dashed across the road to her friend Eva who was in the same shocked state having heard the announcement. Together they went to the war office, and to their relief they learned that only boys over the age of twelve were detailed for the defence of the town. Younger boys were allowed to leave the town with their families. But surely boys even over the age of twelve were far too young to fight? What was happening to their country?

Arm in arm they went home through the eerie darkness that enveloped the town. Since the beginning of the war, streetlamps had no longer been lit because of the blackout.

Back home, Elisabeth started packing quietly, so as not to wake the children. What should she take with her? What would they need? It was winter; therefore warm clothes were the priority. Soon two medium-sized cases were full to overflowing. And she hadn't put any shoes in yet. She just couldn't think straight. Should she fill the big holdall, as well? But how would they manage, carrying all this? Anja was only five, and even Friedrich would be overstretched with big pieces of luggage. She must unpack again and leave behind what was not absolutely essential. After all, it would only be for a short time. Hadn't the newscaster mentioned something about four weeks after which the residents would be allowed to return to their homes?

Suddenly she remembered two little rucksacks she had made some time ago while attending a sewing class. They would be just right for their food for the journey and not too heavy even for Anja to carry.

It was well after midnight when she sank into bed, wondering how to tell her children what was going to happen tomorrow. There wouldn't be any fun in the snow for them. Eventually she fell asleep from sheer exhaustion.

2

Preparing to Leave

When Elisabeth woke up the next morning, Friedrich was already dressed and reading one of his railway magazines. He was a very active boy with a lively mind who never wasted a minute. He was missing school which had been cancelled the week before in preparation for the town's evacuation.

Elisabeth, still in a haze, started preparing breakfast and sat down at the kitchen table with Friedrich.

'Shall I call Anja?' he asked.

'No, let her sleep in today,' Elisabeth said in a choking voice. 'We have to leave this afternoon. I heard the announcement from the loudspeaker last night.'

Friedrich fell silent. He was old enough to understand the situation and to know that this might happen.

'Where are we going?' He looked at her anxiously.

'To Spremberg, to stay with Auntie Hanni,' Elisabeth answered.

Her friend had offered to take them in, if the need should arise. Spremberg was a town in the 'Nieder-Lausitz' area, west of Glogau. She imagined it would take about three hours by train to get there.

As if struck by a thunderbolt, Friedrich suddenly blurted out: 'What about Rudi?'

Before Elisabeth could say anything, he had his coat on.

'I must see him,' he called out to her, running along their hallway and down the stairs.

The two best friends were inseparable and had met up almost daily since primary school. She had often watched them play together with Friedrich's model railway train sets. In recent weeks they had been a real help to her, picking up Anja from kindergarten in the afternoons.

It wasn't long before Elisabeth heard him walking slowly up the stairs and into their apartment. His head hanging, he said in a low voice: 'They've left. Their neighbour told me they went off in the night to stay with Rudi's aunt in the country.'

'Oh, they'll be safe there.' Elisabeth put a confident tone into her voice, to try and comfort him. 'You wait, we'll all be back soon. Come, have your breakfast now.'

To take Friedrich's mind off his worries about his friend, she said: 'Could you then pop over to Oma and Opa, please, and tell them we're leaving at midday.'

Friedrich looked up: 'Aren't they coming with us?'

'No, they are determined to stay on. We discussed this only two days ago. I couldn't persuade them to come away. They say they're too old for such a journey.'

In fact, Elisabeth was most worried about them and couldn't understand why they didn't want to join her. Friedrich looked at her with fearful eyes. Maybe she should be more positive. She said: 'Let's hope it'll all be fine and Glogau will be spared the bombing.'

'And Opa Giertz, is he coming? He's on his own.'

Elisabeth heard alarm in Friedrich's voice. Although her father-in-law had coped admirably as a widower for the last three years, she felt the same concern about him. However, he had made it quite clear that he was not willing to leave Glogau.

'He won't come either,' she replied, 'he says he is an old soldier and maybe they'll need him here.'

'But he can't fight. He's far too old.' Friedrich sounded very upset now.

Elisabeth knew how fond he was of his grandparents. He would miss them terribly. What was this war doing to them?

When Friedrich had left, Elisabeth started making sandwiches to take on their journey. Luckily, the butcher had given her an extra ration of cold meats yesterday. She must also use the cheese up, and there were some oat biscuits she had made last week.

Suddenly, Anja was standing beside her in her pyjamas, bright eyed and clutching her doll, Brigitte.

'Good morning, good morning, oh what a lovely morning,' the little girl started singing, dancing around.

Elisabeth's heart sank. Brigitte! It would be impossible to take such a big doll into an overcrowded train.

She kissed Anja lovingly. 'Come on, sweetheart, have your breakfast. You have to eat well today. We are all going on a journey.'

Anja seemed fascinated: 'On a journey?'

'Yes, we are going to visit Auntie Hanni for a while – you remember her?'

'Is she the one who gave me the big bear book?'

'That's right.'

'Why are we going there? Is it her birthday?'

'No, it isn't. But we have to leave here because there is a war on. Soldiers will be fighting in the town and it

7

would be too dangerous for us to stay here.' Elisabeth could see how puzzling her words were for Anja.

'When are we coming back?' Anja asked

Elisabeth hesitated. She couldn't say for sure when they would be allowed to return. Would they ever come back? But she had to be positive for the sake of her children. She said: 'In four weeks, when the fighting will be over.'

'Oh, Mummy, I want to go to kindergarten. Susi will be waiting for me.'

'Well, darling, I told you kindergarten is closed for a while. All the people of Glogau have to leave, and we have to catch a train this afternoon. Friedrich and I have packed the cases with all our warm clothes.'

Anja was getting more and more agitated. 'I must take Brigitte with me. Have you got a case for her?'

Elisabeth had been dreading this question. 'I'm sorry, Anja, Brigitte will have to stay behind. We have so much to carry. There won't be any space for her.'

Holding her doll tightly in her arms, Anja looked up at her mother. Tears began to trickle down her rosy cheeks: 'But I can't leave her here. She'll be so lonely. Mummy, I want to take her, please!'

Elisabeth hadn't experienced such heartache before. She was a down-to-earth person, certainly not sentimental, but this was almost beyond her inner strength. She knew she had to be firm. Folding her arms around her little girl and the beloved doll she sat down with them, stroking their hair gently, and said: 'Look, darling, I'd love you to take Brigitte. But you'll see, there'll be so many people with all their cases, pushing and scrambling for a place in the train. I know Brigitte would be crushed and torn. She might even fall to the ground and get trampled on. Here, she'll be safe and she'll be waiting for you when you return. Can you understand?'

Seeing Anja stroking the doll's beautiful hair almost brought tears to Elisabeth's eyes now. How she hated causing her such distress.

Anja calmed down slowly. Wiping her tears from her face, she asked: 'Can I take little Kitty then?'

Elisabeth forced herself to sound optimistic. 'Oh, yes,' she said, 'I'm sure you can. Now, let's go to your room. You can put Brigitte in her pushchair.'

While Elisabeth tidied up, she watched Anja as she got her beloved doll ready, combing her hair, changing her into her 'best' dress, and then putting her carefully into the little pushchair, tucking her up in a pink and white blanket. She placed her close to her own bed, and Elisabeth heard her say: 'Now you keep watch over everything, my darling. I'll be back in four weeks.' Turning to her mother she asked: 'Won't I, Mummy?'

'Oh, I hope very much.'

However, although Elisabeth encouraged Anja to believe that they would soon be saying hello to Brigitte, she wondered whether this might not be a final goodbye.

When they were almost ready to go, Oma and Opa came to see them off. Elisabeth was grateful to have their help with carrying the luggage. The distance to the station was not very far, but they had to be careful not to slip on icy pavements.

She couldn't help feeling anxious about leaving her parents behind.

'You should have come with us,' she said to her father who was walking beside her.

'Oh no, my dear,' he sounded so confident, 'we'll be all right. Don't you worry.'

'But haven't you heard there may be fighting in the town?'

'Yes, but they'll leave us old people in peace, I'm sure.'

'What about food? The shops might close down?'

Her mother, who was walking in front with the children, turned round and said with an almost cheerful tone in her voice: 'We've stocked up ever so well. Don't be concerned, we won't starve.'

Elisabeth wasn't convinced, but there was nothing she could do now.

When they got near to the station she was horrified to see huge crowds of travellers. So they decided it would be best to say goodbye quickly at the entrance door.

'Take care, and let us know when you arrive in Spremberg,' Oma said.

'Of course, I will.' Elisabeth replied.

They all hugged each other, and while the grandparents stood and waved to them, with tears in their eyes, Elisabeth and the children worked their way to the ticket counter.

3

Journey to Spremberg

As she knew her destination, Elisabeth was able to purchase tickets for the three of them. Most people had been told that they would be taken to an evacuee camp for the time being.

Anxiously holding on to each other and their luggage, Elisabeth and the two children slowly proceeded along the gangway from where staircases led down to the platforms. Their train was waiting on platform 3.

Friedrich sprinted ahead looking for empty seats through the windows of the train. Now he was calling: 'Come here! Quickly!'

Elisabeth and Anja ran and they all clambered up the high steps into the train, dragging their cases inside. Friedrich had indeed found them good seats, although not at a window, with Elisabeth and Anja next to each other and Friedrich opposite them.

More and more people were pushing in behind them, with everyone squeezing their bulky luggage either under their seats or in racks above their heads.

In the end they found themselves squashed together like sardines in a tin, even more so because they all kept their thick coats on in the cold train. Would it warm up when the engine started on leaving, Elisabeth wondered?

The seat was much too high for Anja, and with her heavy winter boots she wriggled around to make herself more comfortable. Suddenly the lady next to her burst out in anger: 'This girl has trodden on my feet three times now. Can't you keep still?'

Elisabeth was as shocked as Anja, and she apologized immediately: 'I'm terribly sorry. I didn't realize she hit you with her boots.' She pulled Anja closer to herself and said in a firm voice: 'Please, sit still, Anja!'

'Yes, Mummy. I didn't do it on purpose. I'm sorry.' Anja glanced shyly at the angry lady, who looked the other way and wouldn't answer.

This outburst had made Elisabeth feel quite embarrassed and agitated. Hers were the only children in this compartment and she was certainly anxious that they shouldn't be a nuisance to the other passengers. Surely, the train would be full up by now and must leave any minute? She checked the time on her gold wristwatch. It was coming up to two o'clock. They had been here for a good hour already.

Outside on the platforms, Elisabeth could see people rushing to and fro, looking bewildered, calling to their families to stay together in the crowd. Station and military personnel were directing people on to their trains, shouting and pushing them forward.

Elisabeth was holding Anja's hand. It was so cold. 'Shall we have something to eat?' she whispered to her.

'Oh, yes, please, Mummy, I'm very hungry.'

'So am I,' Elisabeth agreed, 'and Friedrich will be, too.'

Reaching for the little rucksack that Anja had bravely carried on their walk to the station, Elisabeth glanced at the unfriendly lady who now sat with her eyes closed. What a bitter look she had on her face. To be sure that Anja wouldn't annoy her again, Elisabeth quickly swapped places with the child.

Even in the rush this morning Elisabeth had, as usual, drawn funny little pictures on the sandwich wrappings, to amuse her children. There was a smiling train engine for Friedrich and a little doll for Anja that made her laugh: 'Oh, Mummy, she looks like Susi with her curly hair! I must keep this and show her when I get back.'

'Yes, you do that, darling. Now eat quietly and don't make a mess.'

She noticed that an old gentleman was watching them from his corner seat by the window. Suddenly he stood up and reached for his bag: 'I'll follow your example. I'm getting hungry, too,' he said, smiling at the children and Elisabeth. 'I bet my wife hasn't put such nice pictures on my packet here. Trudel, are you still there?' he called out, knocking on the thin partition behind his seat. They had become separated while boarding the train.

'Yes, Wilhelm, I'm still here. Are you OK?' Elisabeth heard her answer.

'Yes, dear, just having a sandwich.'

'Oh! Hungry already, old man?' Trudel called back, causing laughter all around.

Elisabeth was relieved that the initial tense atmosphere in the carriage was getting more relaxed and people were starting to chat. How many hours would they have to be in each others' company?

It was 5 o'clock when the train started moving at last.

Having left the town, the train gathered speed, carrying them through the wide, snow covered countryside. In the distance, Elisabeth could see the familiar forests, their tree tops drenched in a reddish-pink light from the rays of the setting sun.

Would they be able to walk there again one day and pick blueberries – their favourite summer fruit? She thought of the delicious dish of yeast dumplings in blueberry sauce her mother would regularly make for them at the height of the season. She couldn't help smiling to herself, when she pictured the family sitting around the table with 'blue' mouths after the meal.

Suddenly the train ground to a halt, stirring some people out of their nervous slumber. There was no station in sight. Elisabeth looked around at the other passengers. What was happening?

'Probably signal failure,' she heard a rough voice say in the next compartment. 'We can't have done more than thirty-five kilometres.'

Anja looked up at her mother anxiously. 'Have we got to get out now?'

'No, not for a long time yet,' Elisabeth answered.

And a long time it would be, with the train stopping and starting and more people cramming in with their luggage. There wasn't enough seating space. Elisabeth could see how weary people looked sitting on their cases in the gangway.

At times the few lights in the compartment went out, leaving them in total darkness for a while. Elisabeth was glad that Anja had dropped off to sleep, pressed between her and the woman who was so terribly concerned that the little girl shouldn't tread on her feet.

Friedrich sat opposite them, in a similarly cramped position. Elisabeth saw him watching everything. He was certainly alert to what was going on around him. She was surprised how much resilience and patience he was showing. This journey couldn't be much fun for him. And yet, she hadn't heard one word of complaint. She was proud of her son.

It was midnight when the train pulled into the station of Cottbus, where most of the passengers had to change trains. It took a long time before everyone had scrambled out and slowly moved to the station waiting rooms, which were soon full to overflowing. Elisabeth took Anja inside, while Friedrich insisted on staying on the platform to watch over their luggage, until their next train came in.

After a long wait at Cottbus station and a few more hours' train ride in the same squashed conditions, the three travellers reached their destination in the early hours of the next day.

Spremberg – coat of arms

The town of Spremberg was only just waking up.

Coming out of the station building, Elisabeth looked around to orientate herself. She had only been here once before, a long time ago, but she couldn't remember where her friend's street was. She asked several people before someone was able to give them directions. How weary she felt after a sleepless night. And the children looked so tired, too. She kept telling them to be careful on the icy pavements. Their cases were weighing down on them heavily.

15

Friedrich was the first to spot the apartment block in Bergstrasse. It was large with several storeys, not too different from theirs in Glogau. Going in through the big communal entrance, they found Auntie Hanni's name on the door of one of the ground floor flats.

Elisabeth rang the bell, her heart racing. What would her friend say when she saw them here? But there was no answer. Surely, she wouldn't still be asleep? It was almost 8 o'clock. Friedrich pressed the bell again – to no avail.

'She must have left for work early,' Elisabeth said looking around in the spacious entrance hall.

Suddenly they heard a door being opened on an upper floor. A middle-aged woman came down towards them. She wore slippers and a long thick dressing gown and was hurriedly smoothing her hair with one hand.

'Can I help you?' she asked with an enquiring look on her face.

When Elisabeth explained who they were, her face lit up.

'Oh yes, Hanni has told me about you. I am Frau Lehmann. Hanni and I are good friends.' Smiling brightly, she shook hands with them all.

Elisabeth sensed what a pleasant person this Frau Lehmann was. She could well imagine what a good friend she'd be to Hanni.

'I'm afraid Hanni was called away yesterday to assist with a Red Cross transport of refugee children. She will probably be back tonight. I'll just get the key to her flat.'

She quickly ran upstairs and then helped them carry their luggage into the small attractive flat. Friedrich and

Anja immediately sat down on the big case together, subdued and hardly able to keep their eyes open.

Looking at them pityingly, Frau Lehmann said: 'I was just making a bit of breakfast when you arrived. Your mummy can come up with me and bring something down for you, all right? You must be starving.'

Walking through Frau Lehmann's spacious first floor flat, Elisabeth was struck by its similarity to her own home. Would she ever see that again?

'I'm sorry we are barging in on you like this,' she said apologetically.

But Frau Lehmann wouldn't hear anything of it. 'Oh, please, don't worry. I'm only too happy to help you out a little. How long have you been travelling?'

Elisabeth told her briefly about their hasty departure and the long arduous journey on the train. Frau Lehmann shook her head in disbelief. 'What a terrible time you've had. You must be so exhausted. Now, look, here is some milk and bread for the children. And I'll make a strong cup of coffee for you.'

'Thank you, Frau Lehmann,' answered Elisabeth. 'You are so kind. I will make up for this later.'

'Don't mention it. It's the least I can do.'

The warmth in Frau Lehmann's voice and her readiness to help was a great relief to Elisabeth and took away much of her anxiety.

When she returned to the downstairs flat with a little breakfast tray, both Friedrich and Anja lay stretched out on the carpet – fast asleep.

Elisabeth sat down in an armchair watching her children. They looked so innocent and peaceful, breathing calmly. What would life be like for them from now on? Would this town become their new home?

She must contact Ludwig immediately so that he knew where they were. She thought of her parents and father-in-law. Shouldn't she try again and persuade them to join her here? Frau Lehmann seemed such a nice person. Surely, she would be willing to help. Elisabeth would talk to her later.

With all these thoughts going through her mind she fell asleep in the armchair.

4

With Frau Lehmannn – at Bergstrasse 8

Elisabeth woke with a start. There was a knock on the door. She jumped up and opened it. It was Frau Lehmann, saying: 'I hope you've had a good rest. I've made you some lunch.'

'Oh, thank you. How kind of you. Is it lunch time already? I must have slept very deeply. Look, the children are still sleeping.'

Frau Lehmann smiled when she saw Friedrich and Anja lying on the floor: 'The poor things, they must be so exhausted after their long journey.'

While they were speaking the children started stirring.

'Come on, wake up, you two,' Elisabeth called, 'we're going to have lunch with Frau Lehmann.'

Slowly, they came to and Elisabeth could see their bewilderment as they looked around the unfamiliar room.

Frau Lehmann led the way upstairs and soon they sat at her dining table, enjoying a meal of potatoes, carrots and a slice of ham.

'This is so welcome,' Elisabeth said, 'you must let me pay for it.'

'Oh, I won't hear of that. It's lovely for me to have your company.'

Elisabeth watched Frau Lehmann smiling at the children, encouraging them to eat enough. She certainly had the ability of drawing them out and winning their confidence quickly.

After the meal Frau Lehmann said to Elisabeth: 'I have been thinking how we shall proceed from here. As you see, I have a big flat. I can easily put you up in my guest room.'

'Are you sure?' Elisabeth asked.

'Yes, of course. Come and have a look.'

The room was large with two beds and a settee. They would certainly be comfortable here, Elisabeth thought.

'Well, this is wonderful. Thank you, Frau Lehmann.'

'I'm so pleased I can help you. We are both Hanni's friends and she will be happy, too.'

In no time Frau Lehmann had helped them carry their luggage up from downstairs and the three of them started unpacking immediately.

While Elisabeth tidied the room up, Friedrich and Anja went to the kitchen, where they seemed to have a lively conversation with Frau Lehmann. Elisabeth listened. Were they talking about 'Oma and Opa'? Yes, she had heard right. She went to join them and saw how concerned Frau Lehmann looked, as she said: 'I hear your parents are still in Glogau?'

'Yes, they didn't want to come with us. I'm really very worried about them.'

'Well,' Frau Lehmann sounded most sympathetic, 'if you can persuade them to come, they are welcome to stay in my son's room.'

Elisabeth was stunned: 'Do you think that would be possible?'

'I'm quite sure. Come, I'll show it to you.'

As she followed Frau Lehmann to the far end of the hallway, Elisabeth sensed that her hostess was becoming somewhat emotional. She wondered where her son was.

Probably at war? Had something happened to him?

Frau Lehmann slowly opened the door. Turning to Elisabeth she said: 'I haven't touched this room since Albert's death four years ago.'

Elisabeth was shocked to hear this: 'Oh, Frau Lehmann, I'm sorry.'

Frau Lehmann continued in a sad voice: 'He was first sea officer on the *Bismarck*, and you will know what happened.'

Elisabeth nodded: 'Yes, it was sunk in battle.'

Frau Lehmann seemed close to tears now: 'The whole of the ship's company perished.'

Elisabeth shook her head. She felt deeply for her as she watched her looking around the room, at the pictures on the wall and the books in the shelves. She followed the direction of her hand as she pointed to a photograph on the desk: 'This is Albert.'

A smart, young man in naval uniform seemed to be smiling at Elisabeth from the picture.

Frau Lehmann explained: 'The photo was taken on his last leave in 1940. He died in 1941.'

Looking at it, Elisabeth was lost for words. She could only guess at the heartache this mother must be enduring.

'But I know for sure that Albert would be happy if his room could be used to give shelter to people in need.' Frau Lehmann's voice now sounded composed. 'So, if your parents decided to come, they'd be most welcome here.'

'I do thank you very much,' Elisabeth felt a great sense of relief. 'I'll try my best to persuade them.'

In the early evening Elisabeth heard the door bell ring very loud – not just once but several times. Someone was demanding to be let in urgently. And who would that be – but Hanni! She must be back from her assignment with the Red Cross.

With a joyful Hello she was greeted by everyone, and the two friends fell into each other's arms.

'Elisabeth, I'm so glad to see you all here, unharmed,' Hanni said. 'Hello, Friedrich! Hello, Anja! Haven't you both grown!'

Hanni was holding something under her arm. She said: 'I knew I had intruders when I found this on the floor in my lounge.'

Elisabeth laughed: 'Oh, that's my scarf. I put it over Anja when we all slept in your lounge.'

'You slept in my lounge?' Hanni looked intrigued.

Anja was quick to explain: 'Yes, Friedrich and I slept on your carpet. We were very tired when we arrived this morning.'

'And now we're going to stay in Frau Lehmann's guest room,' Friedrich added.

Elisabeth noticed the puzzled look on Hanni's face, when she said: 'So everything seems to be arranged here?'

'Yes,' Frau Lehmann said, 'and I have encouraged your friend to let her parents come, too. They can have my son's room.'

'Oh, Berta, that's so kind of you.' Hanni said, and turning to Elisabeth: 'There you have our Frau Lehmann, always ready to help. What about your father-in-law, Elisabeth? He could have my little spare room.'

Elisabeth was quite overcome with all their kind offers of help. However, she was doubtful about Opa

Giertz: 'I don't know if he could be persuaded to leave Glogau. He was very insistent about staying on. He firmly believes that the Russians will be driven back by the German army.'

'Oh, Elisabeth, I don't believe that.' Hanni sounded very sceptical: 'It appears the Russians are approaching fast from the East. Glogau is in great danger. It might be bombed, even.'

Elisabeth was shocked to hear her friend speak in this way:' Do you think I ought to go back myself and get my parents out?'

'Yes,' Hanni was quite firm in her reply, 'I would strongly advise you to do so. You should go back straight away and bring them here. Perhaps Friedrich could go with you.'

Elisabeth agreed: 'You're right. We'll do that. We can take the cases we've just emptied and bring more clothes with us.'

'What about me? Can I come, too?' Anja asked with a rather alarmed look on her face.

'Well, darling,' Elisabeth said, 'I think it would be better if you stayed here with Auntie Hanni and Frau Lehmann. It's such a long journey, and you know how tired you were on the trains.

Anja looked very anxious. But Auntie Hanni came to the rescue with a wonderful idea.

'Do you know, Anja, I have to visit our children's home tomorrow. Some of the children whom I met on the last Red Cross transport are staying there, and I want to see how they've settled in. Do you think you would like to come with me and meet them? You could all play together. They are about your age.'

23

Anja smiled, uncertain, and looked to her mother for reassurance.

Elisabeth nodded encouragingly: 'Anja, wouldn't that be lovely? You've missed your Kindergarten so much. Oh, Hanni, this is such a relief. Do you think they would take Anja in for a couple of nights?'

'Yes, I'm sure. I know Miss Meyer and Miss Neumann very well. They are lovely, very motherly ladies.'

'Are there many toys in the playroom, Auntie Hanni?' Anja asked, visibly warming to the prospect of staying with other children.

'Yes, they have masses, and a wonderful big dolls' house. I'm sure you'd like it there.'

So, all was settled. Elisabeth quickly packed a bag for Anja to take to the children's home and got everything ready for her departure with Friedrich the next day.

5

Return Journey to Glogau

Early in the morning, now carrying their empty cases, Elisabeth and Friedrich boarded the east-bound train. When they asked for train tickets, an official waved them on: 'Not needed any longer.' Elisabeth looked at him in disbelief. Had it come to this?

The journey took them the whole day. Again and again the train stopped for long periods. Sometimes the sound of air raid warnings wafted eerily from the distance, making them shiver in their almost empty compartment. What kind of mission would the other passengers have, travelling eastwards?

Glogau – station

Darkness had fallen when the train slowly pulled into Glogau station. As they walked out of the building, silence hit them. They quickly made their way through the empty streets to the house of Elisabeth's parents.

Oma and Opa were surprised to see them, but Elisabeth sensed how pleased they were.

25

'You have come back quickly! What is happening?' Opa called out.

Elisabeth explained: 'We have come to take you to Spremberg. You can't remain here on your own any longer. It's getting too dangerous. Hanni's friend, Frau Lehmann, has invited you to stay in her flat together with us. She is a lovely lady. So, do pack everything tonight. We have to leave tomorrow by midday at the latest.

Oma was stunned. 'Have we really got to leave that soon?'

'I'm afraid you have to, Mother. The Russians are approaching this town. You must be ready tomorrow. We will also quickly go to Opa Giertz and ask him to join us. Hanni would have a little room for him to stay in.'

'Oh, but have something to eat before you leave here. Friedrich, you look so pale. I'll quickly heat some soup up for us all.'

So they sat around the table, and Elisabeth knew in her heart that it would be their last time in the grandparents' home.

Afterwards Elisabeth and Friedrich walked the short distance to the other grandfather's house. He was equally surprised to see them back so soon. However, when Elisabeth suggested that he should travel with them the next day, he replied quite firmly: 'No, my dear, I will hang on here for the time being. This morning I had a letter from Ludwig. He writes that he has certain information about an imminent counter-attack by the German army against the invading Russian troops. I'm setting my hopes on that.'

So they said goodbye, wishing each other the best of luck. Walking down the stairs Elisabeth wondered when they would see her father-in-law again.

Exhausted, but full of anticipation Elisabeth and Friedrich entered their home once more. The large flat felt very cold. They quickly lit a fire in the bedrooms and started packing again. There was so much they wanted to take but had to leave behind. When Friedrich got his skates out and looked at his mother with pleading eyes, she gave a sigh, saying: 'All right, put them in the bottom of the big case.' How could she deny her boy this little pleasure, when there would certainly be a frozen pond in Spremberg for him to skate on?

She also went to get one of Anja's small dolls which would fit into her own bag. She choked when she stood and looked at Brigitte sitting by Anja's bedside and all the other toys that had given her little girl such pleasure. Was it really true that they had to leave all this behind – their whole home where they had been so happy? Why was this happening?

In the stillness, a strange sound from far away wormed itself into Elisabeth's consciousness. Suddenly she knew: it was gunfire. The Russians were indeed on their way. There was no time to be lost. It was her duty to get her family out of the town. She quickly rechecked the wardrobes and chests of drawers, choosing whatever she thought would come in useful.

Soon their cases were full again and closed. Lifting them, Elisabeth realised how heavy they were. She looked at Friedrich in dismay. But he had a good idea: 'Can't we take our sledge and pull it to the station tomorrow morning?'

'Yes, we could,' Elisabeth said, 'you're right. Perhaps we can even take the sledge on the train. There won't be many people travelling. They've all left.'

She couldn't have been happier about Friedrich's suggestion, for when she woke up in the morning, she saw that the streets were white with snow.

They carried their luggage down and loaded it on the sledge. Then Elisabeth went up again to have a last check through the flat. Looking into each room, she said a silent farewell. Would she ever return? Holding back her tears, she quickly turned the key in the door and walked downstairs. She could hear her own footsteps echoing eerily in the empty building. Friedrich was waiting by the sledge. She saw him looking up to their flat. What thoughts were going through his mind? Was he hoping to come back one day? Her heart ached for him. He so loved his home town Glogau.

Together they pulled the sledge to the station, where the grandparents were already waiting for them. How sad they looked. Elisabeth imagined that they too, were wondering if this was a final goodbye.

Soon they were on their way – unfortunately without the sledge which wasn't allowed on the train. After a long and tedious journey with several changes, they arrived in Spremberg in the evening, tired but relieved to have escaped their endangered home town.

6

Life at Bergstrasse 8

Elisabeth's first port of call the next morning was the children's home, to collect Anja.

The sun was shining, the air felt fresh and crisp, and there was still quite a lot of snow on the trees and the ground; a lovely winter's morning.

Elisabeth enjoyed the short walk through the pleasant streets. People were going about their business, some carrying slim shopping bags. In front of a butcher's shop she could see a long queue of women, chatting to each other. Word must have got round that there was some meat on offer.

Elisabeth would have to find out where to get provisions for her family here. How relieved she felt to be lodging with kind Frau Lehmann, who was so willing to help with everything. Last night, when Friedrich had been sick from exhaustion she had administered him a soothing medicated drink which helped him sleep right through the night. He was still looking pale this morning, sitting up in bed, but he said he felt much better.

She would also have to go to the police station to get registered. How strict the German law was. You were required to sign on within seven days of arrival in a new place of residence. In war time this registration was of course particularly important as only registered residents were entitled to receive food vouchers.

Now Elisabeth could hear voices from the children's home. When she walked through the garden gate she saw that the children were making a snowman in front of the house. Anja was running around with the others, all wrapped up warmly in coats and colourful woollen bobble caps. Together with the two nursery ladies they were so absorbed in their occupation that Elisabeth stood there unnoticed for a few seconds, before a little boy spotted her and called out: 'Look, we are making a snowman. I have a carrot for his nose!'

In an instant, Anja had seen her mother and came flying into her arms.

'Mummy, Mummy, I'm so happy you are here. Where is Friedrich?'

'He is at Frau Lehmann's', Elisabeth replied, hugging her little daughter lovingly. 'And Oma and Opa are there, too. They are looking forward to seeing you.'

'Oh, yes, let's go to them!' Anja could hardly contain her excitement.

One of the ladies came forward to greet Elisabeth.

'So you are Anja's mummy. Did you have a safe journey? We were concerned about you, when Frau Behrend told us that you were travelling back east.

'Thank you,' Elisabeth answered, 'all went well. I'm very grateful that we have found a refuge here in your town. And thank you for having Anja for the two nights. I hope she has behaved herself?'

'Oh, she's been no trouble at all,' Miss Neumann answered, 'we all love her and are sorry to lose her so soon.' Turning to Anja, she said: 'You can always come in during the afternoons for playtime. Would you like that?'

'Oh, yes, please, Miss Neumann. But I want to go home with Mummy now and see Oma and Opa.'

'Of course you do. I'll get your bag ready for you.

And I'll put the beads for your necklace in. You can finish that at home, all right?'

On their way back, Anja bubbled over with excitement, telling her mother about all the things she had been doing at the children's home.

'I can ride the rocking horse. It is ever so high. I was a bit frightened at first, but Miss Meyer held my arm, and then I could do it on my own. I made a nice necklace for you. I'll give the other one to Oma, when I get it done. Miss Neumann taught us how to make cookies. We cut them out on the big board. There were lots of funny shapes.' Anja chuckled.

Elisabeth listened intently to Anja's chatter, very relieved that her little girl had spent such a good time at the children's home, and moreover, that she herself had returned safely with the others. What would have happened to Anja, if their train had been bombed and they had perished? Holding Anja's hand tightly, Elisabeth pushed that thought firmly out of her head.

When they got to the apartment block, Anja ran up the stairs and pressed the bell impatiently. No sooner had Frau Lehmann let them in than Oma and Opa stepped out of their room, delighted to see their little granddaughter again. Holding her up in his arms, as he always did, Opa said: 'Now tell us what you have been up to, sweetheart.'

While Anja kept her grandparents entertained, Elisabeth's concern was for Friedrich, who had gone back to sleep.

Seeing Elisabeth's worried face, Frau Lehmann said: 'He'll be all right. He needs a lot of rest now after all he's been through recently.'

'Thank you, Frau Lehmann.' Elisabeth closed the door to the room where Friedrich was sleeping . 'I can't tell you how grateful I am that we can all stay here with you.'

'Oh, it does me good to be able to help you. I think you all need a long rest today. So, we had better get some lunch. Perhaps you can help me get it ready?'

'Of course, I will, with great pleasure. And later you must tell me where I can do the shopping.'

The two women set to work in the kitchen, and by one o'clock Frau Lehmann's new family, including a rather sleepy Friedrich, sat down to a simple meal of mashed potatoes, cabbage and sausages. Afterwards they all retired to their rooms for a much needed siesta.

The following days were filled with a lot of activity. Elisabeth was very concerned that her family should not give undue trouble to Frau Lehmann. After all, she had been living on her own for years and must find this sudden 'invasion' quite tiresome. However, she kept reassuring Elisabeth how pleased she was to be of help to them.

'Having your children here, makes me feel young again,' she said.

One day, Elisabeth saw her coming down from the loft, calling out: 'Look, what I've found: a set of board games. I didn't know they were still there. They were Albert's. Now we can all have some fun together!'

The children, and no less the grown-ups were delighted, and many an evening hour was filled with laughter and excitement over snakes and ladders, dominoes and draughts and checkers.

With Frau Lehmann's help Elisabeth quickly familiarized herself with her new surroundings. At the council office in the Town Hall she obtained ration cards for her family and was able to do the food shopping every day.

As in Glogau, she was aware of the loudspeakers in the streets that would constantly issue updated war reports. They didn't sound good, she thought. The Russians were approaching, there was no doubt about it.

Several times, Elisabeth took Anja to the children's home, where she was made so welcome and spent happy hours with her new friends. How quickly her little girl had adapted to her new life here. Elisabeth could not but be grateful.

Auntie Hanni had found a new friend for Friedrich, too. He was called Peter and lived only a few roads away. The two boys met up frequently, skating on the big pond in the park, or just wandering around the streets.

Every time, Friedrich came in with fresh observations. Elisabeth wasn't surprised that he was especially fascinated with the long goods trains that ran through the town at regular intervals. What might they be transporting?

One evening he seemed quite shaken, when he told them what he had seen from Peter's bedroom window. About 150 yards away, in the next garden, there was the shell of a German fighter plane. Peter's mother had watched it coming down with a terrific crash, tearing a large crater into the lawn. There hadn't been any sign of the pilot.

Hearing this, Elisabeth couldn't help feeling uneasy. Would the fighting reach this town, as well? Should they think of moving on further west? She had the address of a Glogau friend who had gone to stay with her mother in Quedlinburg near the Harz Mountains, long before the order for evacuation was given. This friend, called Lotte, had urged Elisabeth to join her there, should the need arise. She had said she would be able to find accommodation for Elisabeth and her children. The thought of taking up this genuine offer was now growing ever stronger in Elisabeth.

One early afternoon, when Elisabeth had fallen asleep after a busy morning queuing for bread, vegetables and meat, she was woken up by the shrill ringing of the door bell. After Frau Lehmann had opened the door, Elisabeth could hear a not unfamiliar voice. She jumped up and rushed out of her room.

'Tante Klara, what happened?'

Klara was the sister of Elisabeth's father and had been living with her brother and sister-in-law in Glogau. She had left her home earlier, to stay with friends in the country.

'Well, Elisabeth, we were advised to leave quickly. It was announced yesterday that the Russians are not far away. As you had given me this address, I made my way here, and I hope I can find somewhere to live.'

The others had heard Klara's voice, as well, and came out into the hall to greet her. Anja, especially, was excited to see her beloved Tante Klara again. Hugging her, she asked: 'Have you brought me some more beads? I'm making necklaces.'

'No, sweetheart, I'm sorry. I didn't have anything like that where I've just stayed.'

Elisabeth was really quite upset by her aunt's arrival. It would mean more pressure on Frau Lehmann. But she needn't have worried. As always, the good lady was able to help.

'I've just met my friend Erika in town this morning,' she said, 'I was telling her about you all. She seemed quite envious and said she wouldn't mind having some company herself. Erika has a big flat. I'll go round quickly and ask her, shall I ?'

Before Elisabeth could say anything, Frau Lehmann was off and within less than twenty minutes she returned with her friend Erika.

'I'll be very happy to have you, Frau Fellmann,' Erika said, when they had been introduced. 'I don't live far from here, so you can always visit each other. Come, let's go.'

Elisabeth was struck by the energetic way friend Erika lifted Tante Klara's case and led her down the stairs. Everyone was waving goodbye and calling 'See you soon'.

Elisabeth smiled at Frau Lehmann: 'You are wonderful, arranging this for us.'

'Not at all,' Frau Lehmann answered, 'it's my pleasure. I know my friend will enjoy the company and your aunt will be very comfortable there.'

'I'm sure she will. Thank you so much.'

Frau Lehmann patted her on the shoulder and said with a smile on her face: 'Let's have a cup of coffee on this.'

Elisabeth watched her walk to the kitchen, as if on air. It must make her feel good to help all these refugees, she thought. She followed her with a thankful heart.

7

Deciding to Leave Spremberg

Elisabeth's feeling of unease concerning the political developments was considerably increased by Tante Klara's unexpected arrival in Spremberg. She had told them that the people at her place were urged to leave, as the Russian Army was advancing further west. Could Spremberg soon be in the same endangered situation?

It was on the morning of 12 February, when she was shopping in town, that Elisabeth overheard a conversation between two elderly women.

'You should leave as soon as possible,' one said to the other, 'you have your daughter to go to in the West. If I had someone, I'd go immediately. The Russians can't be more than 100 km away from here.'

Elisabeth was shocked by what she heard and decided on the spot to leave Spremberg with the children the next day.

Back at the flat, her announcement brought initial consternation and upset. Anja was in tears: 'But I must go to the children's home tomorrow. We are having a party for Ulli. He is six.' She stamped her foot in anger and shouted: 'I don't want to go on those horrid trains again, with all the people pushing me around!'

However, Elisabeth was far too preoccupied with the problems that lay ahead of her to pay much attention to Anja's outburst. Her nerves were on edge. She knew the situation was serious, and she had to take the children to a safer place. Thank God, her friend Lotte had given her the address in Quedlinburg. That's where they would be heading tomorrow.

Her parents fully supported her in her decision, although they were not willing to join her so soon after their journey out of Glogau.

'We feel so "at home" here with Frau Lehmann,' her father said. 'We are old now, and if this is our last residence, so be it.'

Elisabeth's mother agreed: 'Yes, Father is right. We'll stay here.' Being practical she added: 'Why don't you take our big case? It's much lighter than yours and holds more.'

'Thank you, Mother. That's very kind. You hang on to mine. Friedrich can bring it over to your room.'

Friedrich had looked very alarmed when his mother had come in with her news. But without saying a word, he went to get the cases out from under their beds. He started arranging some of his and Anja's clothes in little piles, ready to put in the case, as he had watched his mother do in Glogau.

Seeing this, Elisabeth could not help but be proud of her son. He was mature beyond his years. What would she do without him now?

By the time Frau Lehmann was calling them for the evening meal, the luggage for the three travellers was standing ready in the hall.

'I'll help you make the sandwiches afterwards,' she said to Elisabeth.

'Thank you, Frau Lehmann. The butcher gave me some "Mettwurst" spread today. I know the children like that.'

'And you can have some slices of Edam cheese, too.' Frau Lehmann said, always concerned for the well- being of her new 'family'.

While they were eating, a lovely smell of baking emerged from the kitchen. Friedrich was the first to notice it.

Frau Lehmann smiled: 'Well, I thought you would like to take a bit of cake on your journey, too. I just had enough flour to make one quickly.'

'Oh, Frau Lehmann, you are too kind!' Elisabeth was quite overcome. 'How can we ever return all you have done for us?'

'Now, now, don't mention it. It is my pleasure. I only wish you could have stayed with me longer.'

'Is it your special chocolate cake, Frau Lehmann?' Anja asked, her eyes wide.

'Yes, Anja, it is. I've made it especially for you, because you can't go to Ulli's birthday party now.'

Anja seemed to turn over her thoughts in her mind for a moment, before she said: 'But Ulli should have a piece, too. Can you go and take one for him, please?'

'Yes, I'll do that, of course, dear.'

Looking at Frau Lehmann, Elisabeth could sense her sadness and almost read her thoughts. Surely, she must be wondering if she would ever see the little girl again, who had settled so well into her new life here.

'And I'll paint a picture for Ulli', Anja said enthusiastically, 'I can write his name, too. Miss Neumann has taught us to write all our names.'

Elisabeth was relieved to see Anja much happier now. She said: 'You know, Anja, what we'll do? As soon as the war is over, and it can't be long now, we'll come back and visit Frau Lehmann. And you can go over to see all your friends at the children's home.'

'Yes, Mummy, and then we take a cake and have a party for my birthday. I'll be six then, won't I?'

'Yes, you will, indeed. What a big girl. Now you go and paint a nice picture for Ulli and I'll make the sandwiches.'

Later, while the children slept, the adults sat together discussing last minute essentials. Hanni had joined them after an exhausting day of helping with yet another transport of refugee children. Elisabeth sensed her friend's relief, when she said: 'You're right to have decided to leave quickly, Elisabeth. We really don't know what is going to happen here. I do hope the Russians will pass Spremberg by. But it is best that you go on further west. The trains are still running. I'll come with you to the station in the morning.'

'Thank you, Hanni, and thank you for all you have done for us. We couldn't have had it better in the circumstances. I'm so grateful. I've written to Ludwig to give him our new address. Perhaps you could post the letter for me?'

'Of course, I will. And do let us know when you arrive in Quedlinburg.'

Elisabeth went to bed with a heavy heart, wondering where she and the children would be sleeping the next night. Conflicting thoughts were racing through her mind. Was she right to leave this lovely place? They had felt safe here and been well looked after by a lady who had become a friend the moment they had walked into her home. What if their train was bombed? She had read terrible accounts of people being killed and injured on their journeys.

But the Russians were approaching fast, as many people had told her. Surely, Hanni was right. Her first priority had to be to look after her children.

So she tried hard to put all doubts out of her head and snatch a few hours' sleep before their odyssey continued tomorrow morning.

8

On the Move again

Elisabeth woke with a start just before Frau Lehmann knocked on her door at 6 o'clock the next morning. It took her a few minutes to gather her thoughts before she got out of bed

How would she get through this day – 13 February 1945?

She could hear both Friedrich and Anja breathing calmly in their sleep. She would give them another ten minutes while she got washed and dressed.

Frau Lehmann had laid the table for breakfast and put their sandwiches, neatly wrapped in greaseproof paper, on the kitchen table. She had also filled their big thermos flask with peppermint tea. It would be Anja's task again to carry these things in her rucksack.

The grandparents had got up early, too, and soon they were all sitting at the table in their familiar places. But there wasn't much conversation going on; each seemed to be preoccupied with their own thoughts. The children looked tired and Elisabeth had to be firm to make them eat up their porridge. When would they get a hot meal again?

At 7 o'clock, Hanni came up to accompany the three travellers to the station. After much hugging and kissing and promising that they would soon meet up again, Hanni led the way down the stairs, the others waving goodbye. When Elisabeth looked back for the last time she saw Frau Lehmann wiping tears from her eyes. She would miss the children of whom she had obviously grown very fond and Elisabeth was glad that her parents were staying on to keep her company at this difficult time.

It was still dark and the air was cold and crisp. Luckily it had not snowed in recent days, so the pavements were clear and free of ice.

Soon they were at the station and waiting on the platform.

'I hope we get good seats,' Friedrich said. He was looking impatiently into the direction from which the train would pull in. 'I'll run quickly when the train stops.'

'Oh yes, please', Elisabeth answered.

But her heart sank when she saw that the train was already full to overflowing. Surprisingly, quite a number of people got out. Where would they be going?

Friedrich dashed to the nearest door and forced his way through the crowds. However, there was no way they would get proper seats this time. The compartments were packed, and the three of them had to remain in the long corridor with one little folding seat between them. There was just space to squeeze their luggage beside the seat.

They were looking out through the window where Auntie Hanni was standing on the platform.

'Please, let me know when you arrive in Quedlinburg, Elisabeth.'

'Yes, of course, I will. And do say thank you to Frau Lehmann again for me. I really don't know what we would have done without her.'

'And remind her to take the piece of cake to Ulli for his birthday!' Anja called out. She had climbed onto the big case in order to look out of the window.

'Yes, of course, Anja. I'm going over to the children's home, as well. I'll tell them that you had to leave.'

The whistle blew, cutting through Hanni's last words, and then the train started to move slowly. They waved and called goodbye. Hanni started to run alongside the train, but she had to stop and soon disappeared in the distance.

They kept standing for a while, looking out. With daylight slowly emerging, Elisabeth could make out the contours of hills in the distance. What an attractive countryside this was – more beautiful, she thought, than the vast flat fields and forests of the Oder region of her own home.

Eventually they sat down, making themselves as comfortable as possible in the confined space. Luckily, the heating was on in this train, and being near the door would make it easier for them when it came to changing trains. This would happen in Cottbus, where they had changed over on their first journey. Elisabeth remembered spending a long time in the waiting room with Anja, while Friedrich watched over their luggage on the platform. Would the transfer to the next train be quicker this time?

They reached Cottbus sooner than she had thought and were practically pushed out onto the platform by the people pressing towards the door. Everyone seemed to be heading in the same direction. 'Platform 6', someone called. So they moved as fast as they could, as if on a big wave. Elisabeth was anxious not to let go of Anja's hand, as she dragged the big case behind her. Friedrich walked in front of them, carrying the smaller case.

Somehow they were pushed into the next train by the sheer force of people following, and it seemed a miracle to Elisabeth that they found two seats to share between the three of them. Again, they pushed their cases into the racks above their heads and under their seats, and Elisabeth held the rucksack with their provisions on her lap.

Having settled down, Elisabeth looked at the other passengers. Everyone seemed anxious to hold on to their possessions and make sure they knew where all the pieces were in the compartment. This was all they had now. Home was far away. Would they ever see it again?

The train left soon, to everyone's relief. But it was very cold. Friedrich pointed out: 'That window is not quite closed.'

Several people tried to push it up, but to no avail. It was stuck. So they had to keep their thick coats and hats on to stay reasonably warm over the next few hours. How long would this journey take?

The train stopped in various towns, with people getting on and getting off. Sometimes it was not possible for them to reach the door, when they wanted to leave the train. Elisabeth watched with amazement when a family in her compartment climbed out through the window, the mother being helped down first, and her two children being handed to her like parcels by fellow passengers. Elisabeth was horrified. Would they have to do this, as well?

After many hours the train came to a final stop in the town of Halle. There were no connections to go further west that day. Walking along the platform, the travellers heard an announcement over a loudspeaker that they could spend the night at the nearby station hotel, where accommodation for the refugees would be provided. With many others, Elisabeth and the children made their way to the hotel, happy at the prospect of at least having a roof over their heads for the night.

A large number of the hotel rooms had been prepared in a makeshift way for the refugees. Beds had been put on top of each other to accommodate as many people as possible. Elisabeth and the children were shown into a big room and allotted one such bunk bed to share between them.

'You can sleep on top,' Elisabeth said to Friedrich, 'and I will share the lower bed with Anja.'

However, Friedrich put up firm resistance.

'I'm not climbing up there. I'd rather lie on the floor!' he answered in a defiant tone.

'But Friedrich, what is the problem?'

Elisabeth couldn't understand why her son, who had been so sensible throughout their ordeal, was suddenly making a fuss about sleeping in a different, albeit unusual bed.

A little boy next to them came to her rescue. He was lying in the top bed, and obviously enjoying it.

'Come on,' he called, 'it's fun. I can help you up. You can watch everyone from up here.'

But Friedrich wouldn't hear of it. With a stony face he turned away and was just stepping towards the door, when the air raid warning went off. In an instant everyone jumped up rushing out of the door. Red Cross personnel shouted instructions:

'Go to the end of the corridor, turn right, down the stairs, into the cellar.'

Elisabeth held Anja's hand in a tight grip as she ran, keeping an eye on Friedrich who was in front of them. They were almost tumbling down the wooden staircases from which the carpets had been removed. Stone stairs led down to the cellars.

Long benches had been put up against the walls and everyone dashed to get a seat. There was sparse light from a few naked electric bulbs.

Putting her arms protectively around Anja and Friedrich, Elisabeth felt a sudden sting in her upper arm which made her jump. Looking behind her she realized that she had touched a hot water pipe running along the wall.

'Be careful,' she said to her children and the people around her, 'the water in these pipes must be boiling hot.'

'Thank you,' an old woman answered quietly.

With so many people squashed together in a confined space, Elisabeth found the increasing heat almost unbearable. What if these pipes burst? Had they come all this way to be burnt to death by boiling water in a hotel cellar? Should they have stayed with Frau Lehmann after all?

Fear was growing in Elisabeth. She looked around. People were staring ahead of them. Suddenly she could hear muffled sounds above her.

'Fighter planes,' someone said.

Everyone looked up, helplessly. What might their target be this time? And how long would they have to wait down here?

At last the all-clear sounded. With every step up the cellar staircase the atmosphere among these unusual hotel guests became more relaxed, and everyone was relieved to find their few possessions untouched in the rooms.

Suddenly Elisabeth heard the little boy who had encouraged Friedrich to climb up onto the top bunk, call out: 'Look, the whole sky is red!'

While wriggling around in his bed he had obviously moved the blackout curtains aside a few inches. Everyone strained and stretched to have a look out of the window. The sky was indeed glowing red. People were gasping.

'There must be a whole town on fire,' a woman called out, horrified.

'It can't be very far away,' another one said, anxiously. 'I hope we are safe here.'

People looked at each other, nervously, some too stunned to say anything.

Eventually, however, everyone settled down, and an eerie silence spread across the room. Without saying another word, Friedrich had climbed into his bed, not giving his mother further trouble. Anja was fast asleep when Elisabeth lay down beside her, making sure that her slim leather bag with passports, savings books and money was still in place. Throughout her travels she wore this flat little bag strapped tightly around her waist under her dress, to keep it safe.

Early next morning, a Red Cross helper came into the room and announced in a loud voice: 'Breakfast will be served in the dining room. One Mark for adults, 50 Pfennig for children.'

The tables in the dining room had been arranged in long rows. Elisabeth and the children found seats at one end. She was grateful to be offered hot milk for the children and a cup of coffee – albeit 'Ersatz' – for herself. They were each handed a plate with two slices of rye bread with margarine and jam. Everything seemed well organized.

It was a large room with tall windows, looking out onto a wide, tree-lined street.

Elisabeth noticed the long, claret-coloured curtains. Three crystal chandeliers were hanging from the high ceiling. What a lovely atmosphere there must have been here for peacetime hotel guests. They would have been entertained with soft music from the grand piano, which had been pushed right back into a corner, covered with a thick cloth. Now the room was crowded with agitated refugees, eager to get away as quickly as possible.

'Have you heard the news?' a woman sitting next to Elisabeth asked.

'No, what's happened?'

'Last night, Dresden was bombed, completely razed to the ground in three air raid attacks. There was a huge fire storm, which is still raging, someone said. They heard the news on the radio.'

'That's why the sky was so red last night?' Elisabeth said.

'Yes, of course.'

'But Dresden must be at least 60–80 kilometres away from here?'

'Yes, it is. So you can imagine what an enormous fire it must have been. The whole city was alight.'

Elisabeth was stunned. Dresden – the beautiful city,

where she and Ludwig had spent their honeymoon. She could see in a flash before her inner eye the wonderful places they had visited: The Frauenkirche in the baroque style, the Semper Opera, where they had attended a performance of *Der Rosenkavalier* by Richard Strauss, the magnificent bridge across the river Elbe. She remembered their strolls through the large city park and their visit to the castle, with the Green Vault where the Crown Jewels were exhibited. Had all this been burnt down, reduced to rubble?

For a moment Elisabeth was lost in thought. It was Anja who brought her back to reality: 'Can I have another slice of bread, please, Mummy?'

'Oh, I don't know. I don't think so, darling. I can't see any extra bread. They seemed to have counted the slices out. But we've still got some of Frau Lehmann's sandwiches in the rucksack. You can have one when we get on the train. We'd better hurry now.'

Quickly, they made their way back to the station with all the other refugees. Would they reach their destination today and sleep in a proper bed tonight?

9

Arrival in Quedlinburg

The station was as crowded as ever, with people carrying their belongings in cases and bulging bags. Everyone was looking around nervously, trying to find the right platform. Elisabeth approached an official: 'Can you please help me? I want to go to Quedlinburg.'

'Oh, yes,' the man said, 'get on the train to Halberstadt, platform 5, change at Aschersleben. If you hurry you'll just catch it.'

'Thank you,' Elisabeth called, and once again they hurried along with a stream of people. The train was less crowded, and the three managed to find seats by the window. Soon the train pulled out, and to Elisabeth's relief it went along at a good speed. How many hours would they have to spend travelling today?

Elisabeth felt weary. She hadn't slept much in her bunk bed, lying beside Anja. Luckily, the children seemed to be quite alert. Friedrich was pointing things out to Anja: 'Can you see that hill over there? It looks like a lion's head.'

Anja gazed on in amazement. Elisabeth couldn't help smiling. Friedrich really had a lot of imagination. The landscape they were passing through was certainly delightful. Elisabeth was looking forward to seeing Quedlinburg. She knew it was near the Harz Mountains, a beautiful area, sought after by holiday makers. Would they be able to walk there? Soon it would be Spring. Would the war be over by then?

Elisabeth couldn't help feeling anxious about going to Quedlinburg. What would Lotte, her friend, say when she saw her? She was very nice, but Elisabeth didn't know her all that well. Would they have a similarly warm welcome as in Spremberg?

They reached Aschersleben soon after midday. Here, the station was less crowded. While waiting for their connection, they sat down in the little station café. Elisabeth was surprised at the normality in which things went on here. War didn't seem to have touched these parts of the country.

They were able to order a little meal of potato salad and Frankfurters, and some peppermint tea to go with it.

'And afterwards we can have the rest of Frau Lehmann's cake,' Elisabeth said, to the delight of Friedrich and Anja.

'I hope Ulli had a nice time on his birthday yesterday,' Anja became quite thoughtful. The cake must have jerked her memory of her little friend back at the children's home 'Maybe he had to go into a cellar like we did?'

Elisabeth was taken aback by Anja's words. She said: 'I don't know. But I'm sure he'll be all right.' She hoped that the night's experience had not affected her children too badly.

The last leg of their journey only took an hour and a half. By late afternoon they were walking away from Quedlinburg station, through a wide street with lovely villas on either side. This led to a large square, called Kleers, at the end of which lay Brechtstrasse. There they easily found house number 8. Before they could ring the bell, Lotte opened the door.

'Hello, Elisabeth. I thought I recognized you, walking across the square. How lovely to see you.'

'Hello, Lotte. Well, here we are, three of us. I hope you don't mind.'

'Of course not. I invited you. Look, here is my mother.'

A tall lady stepped into the hall. She wore a long dark-blue dress, with a beige shawl draped around her neck. Thick, greying hair framed her round face, and her blue eyes shone brightly when she greeted the newcomers.

'Hello, I'm Frau Kuhrau. Lotte said you might be on your way. I'm glad you've made it. You are very welcome. Do come in. You must be exhausted.'

'Thank you,' Elisabeth said, relieved to find such a heartfelt welcome in this place.

Lotte was very excited and said to Elisabeth: 'You know, we have already found somewhere for you to stay. It's only a few hundred metres away from here, with a family called Meyerding. They own a printing firm.'

'Oh, Lotte,' Elisabeth replied, 'that sounds wonderful. Thank you.'

No sooner had they all sat down in the large sitting room, than a boy and a girl of roughly the same age as Friedrich and Anja burst in. They stopped in their tracks when they saw three strangers

'Ah, here are Bernd and Ingrid,' their mother called. 'Come over and say hello to our visitors. This is Frau Giertz, and these are her children, Friedrich and Anja.'

They all shook hands, the children looking at each other with curious eyes. Elisabeth was happy that there would be friends for her children here.

Later, over supper, a lot of questions were asked: *How long did it take you to get here? Where were you last night, during the Dresden bombing? Did you have enough to eat? Where did you sleep?*

Bernd and Ingrid sat with wide eyes as they heard about their visitors' adventures.

'Was it strange to sleep in the bunk bed?' Bernd asked Friedrich.

'Oh no,' Friedrich said smilingly,' it was quite good, really. I could watch all the other people before I went to sleep.'

Elisabeth noticed that he avoided her eyes while telling his new friend about his experience. She wouldn't remind him of the fuss he had made in that hotel room.

When they had finished their meal, Frau Kuhrau said to Elisabeth: 'I think it'll be best for you to spend your first night here with us. It is already dark now. I'll go along to no.8 Lindenstrasse, and tell the Meyerding family that you have arrived. It will give them time to get the rooms ready, and tomorrow I can take you there – all right? I won't be long.'

'Thank you so much.' Elisabeth was amazed to see this lady's warm and energetic way of dealing with things. She would surely be a wonderful friend in the future.

When Frau Kuhrau had left, she gave Lotte a hand with the dishes. She said: 'Oh, Lotte, you and your mother are so kind to us. I don't know how to repay you.'

'But, Elisabeth, there's nothing to repay. I'm glad

you came. Here you will be out of danger.'

'Yes, I'm sure. I really didn't feel safe in Spremberg anymore. I only hope we won't get any bombing here.'

'Oh, I don't think so,' Lotte replied, 'the Russians won't come as far west as this.'

She put the dishes in the kitchen cupboard and then beckoned to Elisabeth: 'Come, let's go upstairs now. I'll show you where you and your children can sleep tonight. Perhaps you can help me make up the beds.'

'Of course I will, and then I had better call the children.'

The four new friends were already getting on well. When the two women looked into Bernd's room, they found them all playing with his train set. Friedrich was in his element, and the two little girls watched with fascination as the boys let the trains fly past them.

Looking on to this happy scene, Elisabeth just couldn't believe how well things had turned out for them. What a difference to the previous night. They surely had a guardian angel watching over them.

Soon Frau Kuhrau was back from her little mission.

'All is well. I spoke to Herr and Frau Meyerding and their daughter-in-law, who lives on the top floor. They'll be happy to have you in their house and expect you tomorrow sometime during the morning. We can all accompany you and introduce you.'

Elisabeth was quite overcome: 'I'm so grateful, I don't know how to thank you enough, Frau Kuhrau.'

'Oh, it is quite all right, Frau Giertz. In times like these we have to stand together and help each other. We are lucky to have kept our home, while you have lost yours.'

And then, in her warm, matronly manner, Frau Kuhrau called to the children:

'Now off to bed with you, darlings! Tomorrow you'll have enough time to play. We all need some rest now.'

It wasn't long before the lights were out in that pleasant and welcoming home, and Elisabeth soon fell into a deep sleep.

10

Move to Lindenstrasse 8

The next morning, Elisabeth was happy to see that the weather was dry and sunny. At around 11 o'clock, the three women and four children, carrying cases and rucksacks, walked the short distance from no. 8 Brechtstrasse to no. 8 Lindenstrasse. As the name indicated, this street was lined with lime trees.

The children seemed happy enough, and Frau Kuhrau and her daughter Lotte chatted away easily. Elisabeth, however, felt apprehensive. What would their new hosts be like? Frau Kuhrau hadn't said anything about the Meyerding family apart from the fact that they lived in a large house and owned a printing firm, situated behind their back garden.

When they rang the bell, they had to wait quite a while, before they heard shuffling footsteps approaching. The door was opened by an elderly woman, who looked at her callers with a serious expression on her face. Elisabeth's heart sank. This was certainly not a Frau Lehmann or Frau Kuhrau type of person. The latter immediately came to her aid, saying:

'Hello, Frau Meyerding, here we are. This is Frau Giertz and these are her children Friedrich and Anja. I hope we are not too early.'

'No, no, come in.'

Elisabeth noticed that Frau Meyerding had a slight limp, as she stepped aside and let Frau Kuhrau and the new lodgers pass through into the dark hall. Lotte said she would go back home with her children.

Frau Meyerding opened the door to a large room, facing Lindenstrasse. Elisabeth was surprised to see it so pleasantly furnished. There was a comfortable sofa that could be used as a bed at night. There were two armchairs, and there was a big dining table with four oak chairs around it. Light green curtains, reaching almost down to the floor, matched the attractive design of the carpet.

Elisabeth turned to Frau Meyerding, exclaiming: 'This looks lovely. We will take great care of everything.'

Frau Meyerding's response was a mere 'Mmm', as she went to open the door to a room on the opposite side of the hall, saying: 'Here is the second room.'

This also looked very nice. Elisabeth was happy to see a good-sized wardrobe which would certainly hold all their belongings. There were two beds for the children, and in the middle stood a big table with chairs around it. French windows opened out into a veranda. The large garden with trees and bushes would be wonderful for the children in the spring.

'This room will be lovely for Friedrich and Anja, won't it?' Frau Kuhrau said. She turned to Friedrich: 'You can do your homework at this table.'

Elisabeth felt great admiration for Frau Kuhrau. She seemed to have the knack of getting on with people instantly, always finding the right words.

'And here is the kitchen.' Frau Meyerding was leading the way along the hall, opening the door. Elisabeth saw bright sunlight falling through a wide window onto a large kitchen range. On the opposite side was a neat arrangement of cupboards. The big kitchen table in the middle was covered with a colourful wax cloth. Elisabeth thought she would have to be careful not to spoil the immaculately polished terrazzo floor.

'I will tell you later when you can do your cooking here each day.' Frau Meyerding said in an almost toneless voice.

'Thank you very much, Frau Meyerding.' Elisabeth tried to smile politely.

With a nod and a hardly audible, 'That's it then', Frau Meyerding went out of the kitchen. She quickly said goodbye to Frau Kuhrau, leaving the newcomers to their own devices.

Elisabeth looked at Frau Kuhrau a little helplessly, but Frau Kuhrau smiled: 'I'm sure Frau Meyerding means well. She does have a rather abrupt manner. I think you'll get on with her all right. If you need help, don't hesitate to ask. You know where we are. The children will be seeing each other a lot anyway, I gather.'

'Thank you, Frau Kuhrau, I'm sure you're right. We'll settle in here before long.'

'So I'll say goodbye for now. See you at lunch time.' Frau Kuhrau quickly went on her way.

It did not take long before the cases were unpacked at no. 8 Lindenstrasse. The children were quite excited about their room.

'It's bigger than the one we had at Frau Lehmann's,' Friedrich said.

'Yes, you're right,' Elisabeth answered.

'And we can just open this big door and go into the garden to play,' Anja was delighted and wanted to rush out immediately. But Elisabeth held her back.

'No, don't, Anja. We must first ask Frau Meyerding if she'll allow it.'

Suddenly, there was a knock on the half-open door. A young woman stepped in. She said smilingly: 'Sorry to intrude. I'm the young Frau Meyerding. My mother-in-law has just told me that you had arrived and I wanted to say hello to you.'

'Hello,' Elisabeth replied. She held out her hand to the young woman. 'How nice to meet you. Here are Friedrich and Anja.'

They all shook hands.

'I hope you'll like it here,' Frau Meyerding said with a big smile on her face. 'We've tried to make it comfortable for you. Do let me know if you need anything. I live on the top floor. You are always welcome to come up.'

'Thank you, that's very kind of you.' Elisabeth was greatly relieved to know that there was such a nice person in the house. Surely, she would be her friend soon.

Frau Meyerding said: 'I always help my mother-in-law to get our lunch. We eat early. So you can do your cooking afterwards. Will that be all right?'

'That'll be fine,' Elisabeth answered. 'Today we're invited for lunch at our friends' house. But tomorrow I'd like to start on my own cooking.'

They walked over to the larger room, and Frau Meyerding pointed out: 'I hope you have enough space for everything. I've emptied this sideboard for you, too. Perhaps you'll find it useful.'

'Yes, I'm sure I will, thank you.' Elisabeth was very touched by the care and thoughtfulness of this young woman. She had noticed her rounded figure, an indication that she must be well into her pregnancy. Where might her husband be? Possibly serving in the forces – like Ludwig?

'Now I'd better go,' Frau Meyerding looked at her watch, 'we have to have lunch ready when my father-in-law comes in for his midday break. I'll introduce you to him tonight.'

With this, she quickly left them. And soon it was time for Elisabeth and the children to make their way back to the other no. 8 where they were greeted as old friends. Over a hearty meal, the latest news was exchanged, and then there was no holding back of the two boys. They had to let Bernd's model railway trains run again, while Ingrid was eager to show Anja her dolls and all her other toys.

Grandma Kuhrau settled down to a well-earned afternoon rest, and Lotte and Elisabeth set off into town so that Elisabeth could start on some food shopping.

'It is so nice to have you here,' Lotte began when they were walking through pleasant streets in the sunshine. 'Do you remember the sewing circle in Glogau?'

'Yes, I do,' Elisabeth replied, 'and what came in handy recently were those little rucksacks we made.'

'Oh, of course, I have mine here, too. You must come over soon, Elisabeth. We can do some sewing together. My mother has a sewing machine we can use. The children grow so quickly and always need new clothes.'

The two friends spent a pleasant time, getting to know each other a little more, and Elisabeth was able to buy some bread, cheese, and cold meats for their supper.

In the evening, while Friedrich and Anja were asleep

in their new beds which they seemed to like, Elisabeth wrote two letters, one to her husband Ludwig at his military station, and the other one to her 'family' back in Spremberg, to tell them that they had found a good new home in Quedlinburg.

11

Settling In

After a rather restless night, Elisabeth woke early. It was still dark and she wished she could have slept a little longer in her comfortable sofa bed. Thoughts of all the tasks that lay ahead of her were beginning to race through her mind.

First, she would have to go to the police station to get registered, as she had done in Spremberg. On her walk with Lotte yesterday they had passed the impressive building and Lotte had reminded her to report there as soon as possible. She had also pointed out the Town Hall to Elisabeth where she would have to collect her food vouchers. The weekly market would be held today, a Wednesday, on the market square in front of the Town Hall. Would there be fresh vegetables and maybe some apples or other fruit? They had had so little of this kind of food in recent weeks.

And she must ask about a school for Friedrich. He had gone without lessons for nearly two months now. And Anja should be at a kindergarten. There was so much to think of. Would she cope with all of this in her new situation?

When she got out of bed, she noticed how cold the room had got overnight. It would be the same with the other room where the children were sleeping. There were tiled, coal-fired stoves, similar to the ones they had in their own home in Glogau. They did give off very good heat, but of course had to be fed with coal regularly. Elisabeth would have to ask where the coals were kept. How much would the Meyerdings charge her for them?

She still had some cash, apart from her savings books which she had so carefully carried under her dress during their travels. But how long would the money last? She would probably have to look for a job soon.

There was a gentle knock on the door. It opened just a crack and in the faint light of dawn Elisabeth saw Anja's little face popping round. In an instant she came rushing up to her mother, hugging her.

'Mummy, Mummy! Can I get into your bed?' Without waiting for an answer she jumped on Elisabeth's sofa bed hiding underneath the big feather eiderdown.

'Oh, Anja, you little monkey.' Elisabeth couldn't help laughing. 'Did you sleep well in your new bed?'

'Yes, it's very nice. Friedrich is still asleep. Can I go out and play in the garden today?'

'I don't know about that. We have to go into town this morning'

'Why?'

'We have to tell people in an office that we are now living here. They will give us a little book with stamps so we can buy food. You have seen this in Glogau, haven't you?'

'Y-e-e-s.' Anja didn't quite seem to follow her mother's explanation. 'I'm hungry, Mummy, have you got something to eat for me?'

'Yes, let's get ready and then we'll have some breakfast.'

Friedrich had heard their voices and came into the room, looking quite pale and drowsy. How thin he had

63

become. And his pyjama trousers were far too short. He was certainly growing fast at the moment. Elisabeth would have to keep an eye on his diet.

There was a long queue at the Town Hall office, so Elisabeth allowed the children to go out and look around, giving strict instructions to Friedrich not to stray far and be back in twenty minutes. They would meet by the giant Roland figure at the side of the building.

Quedlinburg – Town Hall

While the queue was slowly moving through a wide corridor towards a makeshift counter marked 'food vouchers', Elisabeth's eyes were drawn to beautiful large wall paintings. What a magnificent building this was. She had already admired the grand entrance portal with its carved-stone pillars on either side.

Suddenly she heard the name 'Glogau' mentioned behind her. She turned round and to her surprise saw a couple whom she vaguely remembered from her home town. They, too, recognized her.

'Well,' the man said, 'we've come a long way to meet here!'

'Indeed,' Elisabeth replied. 'Have you just come from Glogau?'

'Yes, we caught the last train out two days ago. They were going to blow the rail tracks up, to prevent hostile invasion.'

Elisabeth was stunned to hear this news, immediately thinking of Opa Giertz. Would he still be in the town?

'What about the people there? They will be trapped.' She looked at the man, horrified.

'Well, all the civilians are supposed to have left by now. There is a lot of military around in the town, preparing for the defence.'

'Oh, how dreadful. My father-in-law was going to stay on. I haven't heard anything from him.'

Elisabeth was now at the top of the queue and was soon issued with her food vouchers. She said goodbye to her Glogau acquaintances wishing them good luck in their new home, and then quickly left the building to join Friedrich and Anja who were waiting for her outside.

The news about her home town had shocked her terribly, and for the rest of the day she was hardly able to concentrate on what she was doing. Was Glogau really going to be bombed? If only she had persuaded Opa Giertz to come away with them. Would Ludwig have heard about what was happening? She must write to him straight away

12

Oma and Opa Arrive in Quedlinburg

Elisabeth's anxiety about her father-in-law was soon assuaged, when she received a letter from Ludwig which had crossed with hers. The authorities in Glogau had given out final urgent instructions to all remaining citizens to leave immediately, as the bombing of the town was expected any day.

Reluctantly, Opa Giertz had followed this warning and had in the meantime arrived safely in Eschwege, a small town in Hesse, an area Elisabeth had only vaguely heard of. There a friend had given him temporary accommodation.

Whilst she was very relieved to hear of this outcome, the news about the imminent bombing of Glogau left Elisabeth with a growing feeling of unease regarding her own parents' safety. After all, in Spremberg they were not that far away from Glogau. What if the air raids were extended to their area? Some radio bulletins made very uncomfortable listening, indeed.

Here in Quedlinburg, an attractive medieval town at the foot of the Harz Mountains, life was relatively calm. People went about their business, seemingly unaware that the war was still going on. Everything appeared peaceful; Elisabeth never even saw any soldiers in the streets.

With the support of their friends, they were settling into their new home quite well. Elisabeth knew that she could call at the other no. 8 – as they had christened the house – with any problem she might have.

She was happy to see how well their children got on with each other. As the days were growing longer, they were spending more time in the open air. The big square 'Kleers', practically in front of their houses, was an ideal spot for the children to play. They started mixing with other local children who showed them around in their town.

Quedlinburg – Castle & Church

A particular attraction for them was the 'Schlossberg' at the edge of town. Here, a medieval castle and Collegiate church stood on a steep sandstone cliff, overlooking the town. Friedrich had never seen such a place before, and he was very excited when he described it to his mother one day: 'The castle and church stand very close together and a long brick wall runs around them, like a belt. You can walk along the wall and see the whole town beneath you.'

'I hope you didn't try to climb over it,' Elisabeth called out anxiously.

'No, of course not. It's far too high. You just walk inside it. Can we go there next Sunday? I can show you the way.'

'Yes, perhaps we can do that,' Elisabeth replied.

Friedrich was now attending the local 'Mittelschule', together with Bernd. After his initial disappointment of not going to grammar school here, as he had done in Glogau, he was on the whole enjoying it. Elisabeth explained to him that she couldn't afford the grammar school fees and promised that once the war was over and his Dad had returned, he would be able to change back. Anja was happy to go to a nearby kindergarten each morning, returning home with new stories and songs she had learnt.

Elisabeth was amazed how quickly both her children seemed to be adapting to their new life. Had they forgotten their own home by now? Maybe it was just as well. They would probably never see it again. She wouldn't tell them about the expected bombing – not just yet, anyway.

However, the thought that her parents might be in danger didn't leave her. She should encourage them to join her here. Of course, they felt so at home with the kindly Frau Lehmann and would dread another long journey. Maybe her friend Hanni would talk to them and perhaps even come and bring them? One afternoon she made up her mind to discuss the matter with her friends at the other no. 8 and went over to see them.

Frau Kuhrau didn't have the slightest hesitation: 'Of course, you must ask them to come here. We can put them up in a room on the top floor to start with.'

'Are you sure?' Elisabeth asked. She didn't want to put them to more trouble.

'Absolutely. We don't use that room at the moment. There is a small bathroom next to it. And they can use our kitchen for their cooking.'

'Oh, Frau Kuhrau, it would be wonderful. I'd be so relieved. I've been terribly worried.'

'Well, do tell them we'll be very happy to have them.'

A few days later, in the afternoon, Elisabeth and the children were waiting excitedly on the station platform when a long train pulled in. Friedrich soon spotted Oma and Opa with Auntie Hanni, and they all flew into each others' arms – happy to be reunited once again.

While the children kept their grandparents entertained on their walk from the station, Elisabeth was eager to have a chat with her friend: 'I hope I haven't put too much strain on you, Hanni, asking you to accompany my parents.'

'No, not at all, Elisabeth. You were quite right to get them to come here. The situation in Spremberg is becoming very difficult. The food supplies are not good and last week we had a shortage of coal. There was hardly enough to keep one room warm in Frau Lehmann's flat. I think, in a way she was relieved that your parents decided to join you, although she was very sad to see them go. They really got on so well together.'

'I'm sorry for Frau Lehmann. She must be feeling quite lonely again now. Have you any information about air raids? I heard that Glogau is going to be bombed.'

'Yes, that's right. What about your father-in-law. Is he still there?'

'No, he got out just in time; Ludwig told me in a letter.'

'Oh, I'm glad.'

The little group had arrived at the other no. 8 and Elisabeth was very touched to see how warmly her parents were welcomed into the house. She felt a great burden being lifted from her. Surely, Oma and Opa would be happy here.

Early the next morning Elisabeth accompanied her friend to the station. The Kuhraus had put her up for the night. Elisabeth thought she looked very tired.

'Will you have to go to work straight away when you get back?' she asked

'Yes,' Hanni replied, a little resigned, but smiling, 'we're very busy at the Red Cross these days.'

'Oh, Hanni, I hope you're not overworking, I'm worried about you.'

'No need to worry about me, my dear. You know me – I'm a tough nut!'

Elisabeth laughed. Her thoughts went back to the days when they had spent their nursing training together in Glogau. Elisabeth had admired Hanni's energy then. She was always up first and didn't show much tiredness even after a demanding day on the wards.

'But do look after yourself, Hanni. You seem to be working extra hard now.'

'Well, I have to admit, these transports I'm assisting in are quite tiring. But it can't go on forever. The war must be over one day soon.'

'Oh, I hope so,' Elisabeth gave a sigh.

At that moment, Hanni's train pulled in. They embraced each other, and Elisabeth said in a choking voice: 'Thank you again for bringing my parents. I'm so grateful.'

'Elisabeth, it's been a pleasure. I'm so glad they've found a good home here.'

She quickly boarded the train, and after a few minutes Elisabeth was waving goodbye to her friend. When would she see her again?

13

Getting a Job

By now Elisabeth knew her way around in the town and was able to assist her parents on their visits to the various offices and shops.

One morning, while she was waiting at the Police Station for her parents to be registered, she spotted a big poster which read: 'SOS! Nursing staff urgently needed to attend to war wounded. Can you help? Personal applications to Quedlinburg Hospital, please'.

Elisabeth felt excited. As a qualified nurse she would surely be in with a good chance. What an opportunity to earn some money while working in her own field.

Her parents were very pleased for her and offered straight away to help look after the children when she would be out nursing. How fortunate that she had had the presence of mind to bring her State Certificate of Nursing with her from Glogau. She would go and apply immediately.

As she had hoped, she was offered a place and a few days later she began her duty as a night nurse.

At first it felt strange wearing a uniform again after so many years. She had forgotten how long it took to get herself ready. Her hair was now much shorter and she needed more pins to hold the cap in place. But in the dimmed light surely no one would notice that?

With a kind staff nurse assisting her during her first nights she soon got into the routine and was enjoying her work very much. Her patients were mostly soldiers recovering from operations. After she had administered their medication, they normally slept through the night, which gave her time to do the paper work in relative peace.

Although she was relieved by a colleague for two short periods to have a rest, she was on her feet most of the time, and she had to admit to herself that she found the nursing harder now than as a young single woman when she didn't have two children to look after.

However, both Friedrich and Anja were willing to help, and Elisabeth was particularly impressed with the way Friedrich took over a number of tasks, especially in the mornings when she needed her sleep after returning home in the early hours. She always prepared the children's breakfast as soon as she got in and left it on a tray in the kitchen, before going to bed.

When the children woke up, Friedrich would help Anja to get ready, make their tea – taking care not to get in the way of old Frau Meyerding in the kitchen – and carry the tray into their room. They mostly had slices of rye bread with margarine and jam, and perhaps an apple between them. Often there was no milk for the children, and Elisabeth was worried about the effect this lack in their diet would have on their growing bones.

When she got up during mid-morning, the children had left for school and kindergarten respectively. But the breakfast dishes had been washed and put away, the beds were made and the room tidied up. Elisabeth couldn't help but feeling touched. They were such good children, and yet they had so little. Surely, they must miss their own things left behind in Glogau: Friedrich's train set, his books and railway magazines, his modelling kits, and Anja's dolls and little bear and all the other toys. Probably they were all smashed to smithereens in the bombings by now. Oh, this wretched war. How on earth were they going to build up a proper life again? Would Ludwig find them here soon?

But there was no time for lingering on these kinds of thoughts. She had to go out quickly and see what she could get in the shops, in order to put a reasonable meal on the table. On her way into town she would usually pop in at the other no. 8, where her parents had found such good accommodation. As they lived so close by, they were able to visit the family at no. 8 Lindenstrasse quite easily, and Elisabeth was grateful that they could be with the children in the early evenings when she had to go on night duty.

Spring had brought extra warm weather this year, after a long cold winter, and sometimes grandparents and grandchildren accompanied Elisabeth to the hospital before enjoying an evening stroll together. Friedrich seemed proud to be the leader on these little outings, showing his Oma and Opa all the places he had explored in preceding weeks. And Anja, even though she didn't like her mother leaving her, as she would miss her at bedtime, was happy to have Oma and Opa instead. They were good listeners and loved their little granddaughter's chatter about her daily adventures at the kindergarten.

It was now Easter week and the children were making decorations, for example little garlands and colourful paper eggs. They were all going to celebrate together. Oma had saved up some of her food vouchers to buy the ingredients for a cake.

On Easter Sunday, the grandparents took their grandchildren to a family service at the church, while Elisabeth prepared their dinner. She had managed to get a small chicken and some really good potatoes, carrots and cabbage. She also had half a dozen eggs. In the absence of egg colouring she carefully tied brown onion skins around the eggs with pieces of string before she boiled them. That left attractive patterns on the eggs. She would hide them for the children in the two rooms and the veranda. Although the weather was fine, Frau Meyerding would not allow them to step out into the garden, not even for an Easter egg hunt.

After a happy mealtime they all went for a walk in the sunshine. There were a lot of people about in the parks and by the castle on the hill. Everyone seemed to be enjoying themselves. But the conversation between Elisabeth and her parents inevitably turned to the war. Opa was an avid paper reader and was following the events with great concern. When would they be able to return to their beloved home town?

When they got back, Elisabeth switched the radio on so that her parents could listen to the evening news. While she was busy getting sandwiches ready for the family, her attention was suddenly drawn to the newscaster's words: 'After heavy fighting the fortified town of Glogau has fallen today, the first of April 1945.'

Elisabeth held her breath. Glogau – fallen?

'Did you hear?' she called out to her parents.

'Yes,' her father answered, 'but surely, that's not our Glogau? There is another Glogau further east.'

'Oh, no, Father, it is our Glogau all right. I met a couple in town not long ago. They just got away on the last train. They told me that the bombing was expected.'

Her father was shaking his head. She could see that he didn't want to believe what he had heard.

After the news had been repeated, they turned the radio off, and Elisabeth called everyone to the table to have some supper. But in contrast to their happy dinner time, this meal was spent in a very quiet and subdued mood.

The grandparents left soon afterwards to go back to their own place. Elisabeth was glad to be off duty over Easter. So she could be with the children in the evening. Friedrich would want to talk to her. He was growing up fast and seemed mature beyond his years. How would this news affect him?

14

A Surprise Visit

Over the weeks Elisabeth had become very friendly with the young Frau Meyerding, who seemed happy to have another woman in the house to talk to. Soon they were on first name terms and would often chat together either in Elisabeth's sitting room or in Gerda's flat on the top floor.

'This is a very homely place.' Elisabeth looked around admiringly when she saw it for the first time.

'Oh yes, I like it very much,' Gerda replied, 'and the good thing is that I'm independent. You may have noticed that my mother-in-law is not the easiest person to get on with. She can be very quarrelsome. But she never comes up here.'

Elisabeth couldn't help smiling. She had had a few little brushes with the old lady: 'The other day she told me off for leaving an unwashed saucepan in the sink while we were having lunch.'

'Oh, that's typical of her,' Gerda nodded.

'But I like your father-in-law, Gerda. He is very nice and he has a great understanding of children. He took Friedrich to the print house the other day. Friedrich was fascinated and kept telling us all about the big machines there.'

'Yes, old father is all right. He is always the peacemaker. He told me about Friedrich's visit and how interested the boy was.'

As Elisabeth had guessed, Gerda's husband had been drafted into military service, like Ludwig.

One morning she appeared very nervous, when she said to Elisabeth: 'I haven't heard from Hans for several weeks now. I don't even know where he is. How I wish that this awful war was over. I'm expecting our baby in mid-May, and I so hoped that Hans would be back by then.

Elisabeth felt very sympathetic. 'I do understand. How are you feeling these days?'

'Oh, I'm quite OK. I know I can call at the maternity clinic at any time if I need to. It's just across the square from here, very convenient.'

'You must let me know if I can be of help to you, Gerda. I have worked on a maternity ward in the past, albeit a long time ago now.'

In a flash Elisabeth remembered all those newborns she had held in her arms and handed to their mothers for feeding. They would be older than Friedrich by now. Where would they be? Had some of the boys been forced to stay behind and defend the town? She couldn't bear the thought.

'Thank you, Elisabeth,' Gerda replied. 'It's really lovely you came here. I never thought we would have a nurse in the house one day. How are you getting on with your night duty?'

'Oh, fine. Most nights are really quiet. The injuries we see here are not too bad, thank goodness. And these young chaps seem to recover quite quickly. I can always tell by their cheeky remarks when they are getting better!'

Gerda smiled: 'I can imagine that.'

As the days went by, Elisabeth felt a growing anxiety about her husband Ludwig. Their contact had been very good during most of his time away. They were able to correspond regularly through the 'Feldpost', a reliable mail service of the forces.

However, there hadn't been a reply to her last two letters and she was becoming increasingly worried. Where might he be? Ludwig was a "messenger" for the Air Force. This meant that he had to travel a lot. He was sent from one military post to another and could be anywhere in the country. He carried secret messages in a sealed leather bag and also a revolver which he was instructed to use on anyone who might try to take his bag from him. What if something like this had happened and he had been shot at himself? The thought of it made Elisabeth shiver. When would she hear from him or even see him again?

Her anxious waiting came to a sudden end on Saturday 7 April, when in the afternoon, Friedrich who had been playing in the square, came rushing into the house, calling at the top of his voice:

'Look, who is here!'

There was Ludwig – in his blue Air Force uniform.

Elisabeth stood, stunned. And then she flew into her husband's arms and the two of them held each other for a long moment.

'Oh, Ludwig. I've been so worried about you. Where have you come from?'

'Well, I'm officially on a trip from Fürstenwalde, Mark Brandenburg, to Nürnberg. But they gave me permission to take this long detour to see my family. The commandant decided he could justify this favour.

I must have been a good boy.'

'I'm so happy to see you. How long can you stay?'

'Only two nights, I'm afraid.'

Elisabeth was slightly taken aback. 'Oh, I see. But it's wonderful you've found us here. We'll have to make the most of it.'

Someone came running along the corridor and with a loud 'Daddy! Daddy!' Anja rushed into the room and into her father's outstretched arms.

'Anja, my darling.'

Ludwig lifted his little daughter up and kissed her tenderly. Putting her down again he said: 'Look at you – haven't you grown!'

'Yes, and I can do the handstand. Look! Friedrich, help me!'

Before they could stop her she was standing on her hands with Friedrich holding her legs up in the air.

Ludwig laughed out loud: 'Bravo! Well done, Anja. I wish I could do that. They haven't taught me anything like that in the Air Force.'

The excitement at no. 8, Lindenstrasse couldn't have been greater that day. It was exactly four months ago that they had said goodbye to each other at Glogau railway station, and now each of them had so much to tell.

When the children had gone to bed, husband and wife were able to share a few precious hours alone with one another. Their talk soon turned to the recent news about the fall of their home town. Elisabeth couldn't hide her anxiety: 'Do you think we'll be able to go back to Glogau again soon?'

'I don't know. Not in the near future anyway.'

There was a resigned tone in Ludwig's voice: 'From

what I've heard the town lies in ruins, and there are rumours that the whole region of Silesia will be annexed to Poland once the war is over.'

Elisabeth looked at her husband in disbelief: 'So we would be foreigners in our own land?'

'Yes, if you want to put it like that.'

'But what shall we do? Will we have to stay here?'

'Well, we just have to wait and see what the situation will be like. I don't think anybody knows yet what is going to happen.'

Elisabeth fell silent. The thought of having lost her home began to hit her hard.

But then she heard Ludwig's comforting voice: 'Let's just be grateful for what we have now and enjoy these few days together. I'm so relieved you're all well. The children seem very happy here.'

'Oh, yes, it's amazing how well they have adjusted. And of course, it is nice to have my parents here, too. They are a great support.'

Elisabeth noticed a thoughtful expression on Ludwig's face. He said: 'Do you know what I would like to do tomorrow?'

'No, tell me.'

'I would like to go to church. I'm sure your parents will be going; maybe we can join them?'

Elisabeth hesitated slightly before answering: 'Oh, of course, if you would like that.'

In fact, she was quite surprised by Ludwig's suggestion. They had not been church goers in Glogau. As a journalist at the local newspaper Ludwig had considered it wise to stay away from the church for political reasons. He hadn't even attended Anja's christening service. Something or someone must have had a great influence on him recently. What kind of experiences might he have had over the last few months?

'I'll send Friedrich over in the morning to tell my parents and then we can all go to church together. Actually, the children went with them on Easter Sunday and they enjoyed it very much.'

So the decision was taken and it wasn't long before Elisabeth fell asleep in her husband's arms.

15

An Air Attack – observed

When Elisabeth woke from a deep sleep the next morning she was surprised to find herself alone. Where was Ludwig?

Suddenly she heard voices from the other room. The children were chatting to their father.

She went over and found all three of them sitting on Friedrich's bed looking at school books and pictures.

Elisabeth smiled at her husband: 'So they coaxed you out of bed?'

'Ah well,' Ludwig answered, 'I was awake anyway, and then I heard a soft knock on the door and there they both were. I must say I'm very pleased with all the work they've done here.'

Elisabeth agreed: 'Yes, I think they're doing really well. Friedrich has very good teachers at his school. You like them, don't you, Friedrich?'

'Yes, but I would like to go to grammar school again. I want to learn Latin, and they don't teach that at the "Mittelschule".'

Elisabeth was touched to see Ludwig putting his arm around his son: 'I'm sure it will be possible, Friedrich, once the war is over. It can't be long now. Just be patient and do your best at this school.'

'Fräulein Müller is very nice,' Anja chipped in, 'she is teaching us how to paint. Look, Daddy, I did this picture of the castle. You can have it.'

'Oh, thank you, Anja. I like it. Is this castle here in Quedlinburg?'

'Yes, we went there with Fräulein Müller, and then she taught us how to paint it.'

Elisabeth looked at her little daughter with amazement. Here she was, in a strange town, telling her father confidently about her daily life. Surely, her children would pull through – come what may.

After breakfast they all walked to church, having called for the grandparents at the other no. 8.

Elisabeth was astonished to see so many people at the service. And what a surprise to find that the preacher was pastor Fiedler from Glogau. Elisabeth had heard him preach once or twice in the past when on the odd occasion she had joined her parents for Sunday worship at their church. When had he arrived here in Quedlinburg? She must speak to him afterwards.

Sitting next to her husband, Elisabeth could sense how deeply affected he was by the service. He sang with gusto, especially the old Luther hymn, 'Now, Christians, come, rejoice, go forth in jubilation'. Elisabeth couldn't quite enter into this kind of sentiment. In her present situation she certainly didn't feel like rejoicing. However, she had to admit that she and her family had fared much better than many others. She was thinking of the hundreds of refugees from Silesia who had perished in the Dresden bombing while she and her children sat in relative safety in that hotel cellar.

Later, at home, just as Elisabeth was calling her family to lunch, they suddenly heard a wail of sirens from a distance. They all stood still for a few seconds, listening.

'There must be an air attack,' Elisabeth looked at Ludwig in alarm.

'Yes, but it is some way away from here, I'm sure.' Ludwig said with authority in his voice.

'Look, there are fighter planes.' Friedrich had run to the window. They all followed, gazing up into the sky. Elisabeth instinctively threw her arms around Anja. About ten to twelve planes were droning past in the distance.

'They are Americans,' Ludwig seemed to be able to recognize their colour and design instantly.

Elisabeth could hardly bear the sight. Where were they heading? She was about to turn away from the window when she saw two planes exploding in the air – obviously having been hit by German anti-aircraft guns. They fell to the ground in pieces.

She gasped, and in a whispered scream she called out: 'Oh, those pilots!'

Ludwig was by her side: 'They don't stand a chance, I'm afraid. At least they won't have felt anything.'

Elisabeth stood frozen. Those men were dying in the air, while she was looking on. The war was certainly not over yet. Here in Quedlinburg she had felt safe up to now. But today her hope of escaping the bombing was severely shattered. When would the planes come for this town?

Anja brought her back to reality: 'Mummy, are we going to have lunch now?'

'Of course, darling, we must eat before it all gets cold.' Luckily Anja had not seen the exploding planes and seemed her cheerful little self.

While they were sitting at the table, there was a knock on the door. It was Gerda Meyerding.

'I must tell you quickly: the air attack was on Halberstadt, a town only sixteen kilometres away from here. My father-in-law's sister lives there, and he is terribly worried, as you can imagine.'

Elisabeth looked at her in dismay: 'Oh, Gerda, I'm sorry.'

'It was a very heavy attack, the radio newscaster announced a minute ago,' Gerda sounded most upset.

'Please, do let us know about further news.'

'Yes, of course, I will.' Gerda hurried away.

As the weather was fine, the family decided to go for a walk in the afternoon. They called for the grandparents again, who had also observed the air attack.

While they were crossing the square Kleers, Oma said: 'I can smell something burning.'

'Yes, I can, too,' Elisabeth agreed, and so did all the others.

'This smell comes from the burning town of Halberstadt,' Ludwig explained. 'I've experienced this before on my travels. It must have been a terrible attack. I wonder how many people have been killed.'

They looked at each other, stunned. Here they were walking peacefully in the sunshine, and not far away people had just lost their homes, if not their lives.

'Halberstadt is a very interesting medieval town,' Opa said. 'Frau Kuhrau told us it would be well worth a visit.'

'Well, not anymore, I gather,' Ludwig said in a resigned tone.

It was Anja who first saw the little pieces of burnt paper fluttering down on to the path. She picked one up and they could see that it must have come from a newspaper. They could decipher a sentence which read: 'The meeting will be held on Tuesday, 10 April 1945 at Halberstadt town hall.'

Would this meeting still go ahead, Elisabeth wondered.

She could hardly bear to think of the misery that had happened so near her today. The sight of the exploding planes was still vivid in her mind. And tomorrow Ludwig had to leave. Where would he have to go next? When would he be back?

But she had to hide her worries for the sake of the children. They were enjoying their father's presence so much. Anja couldn't wait to show her daddy the castle, which she had visited with the kindergarten group and of which she had drawn that lovely picture.

Half of Quedlinburg seemed to be on their way up to the castle on this beautiful afternoon. The first fresh green was showing on the trees and bushes, some spring flowers were in blossom and the birds were singing happily. However, Elisabeth could sense that everyone was preoccupied with the same thought. She couldn't help overhearing some of the conversations, and more than once the words 'air attack on Halberstadt' were mentioned.

After the walk they all went to the other no. 8. Frau Kuhrau had kindly invited them to supper. Elisabeth was happy that Ludwig would be able to get to know this kind family who had given her and her children, as well as her parents, so much support and practical help in the preceding weeks.

She couldn't believe her eyes when she saw the spread on the dining table. There was a selection of cold meats, sausages, liver paté, cheese and butter and delicious fresh bread; there were even bread rolls.

'Frau Kuhrau!' she exclaimed, looking at her in astonishment.

Frau Kuhrau gave one of her intriguing smiles: 'Well, I hope you will all enjoy this. My friend Irmgard came over from Ströbeck yesterday with this offering from their pig slaughter. She and her husband run a small farm in the village, and every now and then Irmgard comes and brings us some sort of produce. I thought it would be nice to share this with you tonight.'

Everyone was quite overcome, and Elisabeth was happy to have her husband with her to express their thanks: 'Frau Kuhrau, I didn't expect to be invited to a "banquet" on my leave. Thank you for such a wonderful feast. I'm afraid there won't be much left over at the end, with all these hungry mouths around here!'

Frau Kuhrau smiled: 'Oh, it's a great pleasure. A joy shared is a joy doubled. Now, do tuck in, all of you. Bon appétit!'

The conversation inevitably turned to the air raid that had shocked everybody today. Elisabeth could see that Frau Kuhrau was very upset at the mention of the name of Halberstadt: 'That town is very dear to my heart. I studied there at the College of Music and I lived there for several years before I married.'

'Do you think there was a lot of destruction?' Elisabeth looked at her anxiously.

'Oh yes, I fear there was. The radio reports sound awful. The death toll must be very high.'

This day had certainly been one of mixed emotions. Elisabeth was concerned about the effect it would have on the children. She couldn't protect them from the reality of what was happening around them, but neither could she really explain it to them. Her only hope was that this terrible war would be at an end soon.

16

Quedlinburg in Danger

Soon after Ludwigs's visit Elisabeth noticed that the atmosphere in the town was changing. People seemed absent-minded and nervous, often standing around in little groups, talking to each other in low voices.

When she went out shopping one morning she found that the greengrocer's shop was closed. Several women were waiting in front of the door, looking at each other, puzzled.

'What's happening?' one woman asked, 'there's no notice to say why they're closed.'

Elisabeth looked at her in alarm. Where would she get her vegetables? What if other shops were closed, too?

As there was no sign of the shopkeeper, she quickly went on to the baker's. To her relief she saw a queue in front of the shop. At least she would be able to buy bread.

At the butcher's she just managed to get a pound of stewing beef. She rushed on to the general store, where she joined a long queue. The woman in front of her turned round looking at Elisabeth with fear in her eyes, saying: 'There's not much left in the shop. They say they haven't had anything delivered today.'

'Are you sure?'

'Yes, someone said, when the van driver got to the station this morning to pick up the daily delivery, he was told that the trains had stopped running.'

Elisabeth stared at the woman in disbelief. What could this mean? Were they cutting off Quedlinburg in order to bomb it? She couldn't forget about the air raid on Halberstadt, which she had witnessed from a distance a few days ago. She must go and see her parents and her friends at the other no. 8 on her way home.

Luckily, she could buy some flour and sugar and even a few eggs at the store. So she would be able to make a cake for her father's birthday next week. But how long would the food supply last?

When she went into the news agency to buy a daily paper, she noticed that there were none on display. She turned to the news agent, but he said sadly: 'Sorry, no papers today.'

Elisabeth stood there, stunned: 'No papers? But why?'

The man just shrugged his shoulders: 'I've no idea.'

Her parents and her friends at the other no. 8 were just as baffled when they heard about Elisabeth's experience. What was happening to the town?

'I can help you out with some potatoes, Elisabeth.' The ever practical Lotte was already on her way down to the cellar where the family stored their vegetables and everything else that needed to be kept cool.

Coming up, she handed a little bag to Elisabeth: 'Here you are, take this. I put a cabbage in as well.'

'Oh, thank you, Lotte. How will I ever be able to make up for all your kindness?'

'You don't have to make up for anything, Elisabeth. We are your friends, and we want to help you as much as we can. When I go out I'll see if our greengrocer is still open. I'll come round later and let you know.'

'Oh, Lotte, what's going to happen? I thought the war was almost over?'

'Maybe it is. Let's be hopeful.'

A few days later, while Elisabeth was preparing supper in the kitchen, a sudden bang outside made her start. She looked up. Another bang. She knew the sound: machine guns! She ran to the window but couldn't see anything.

'Anja! Friedrich! Are you there?'

Anja came running from the other room where she had been playing. But where was Friedrich?

'He went to see Oma and Opa,' Anja remembered.

'Oh, yes, you're right. I hope he stays with them and isn't walking along the street now.'

A third bang made them jump. With that Herr Meyerding came rushing along the hall, calling out: 'Everybody, come down into the cellar. There is machine gun fire outside. Turn the gas off quickly.'

Elisabeth took Anja by her hand and followed the Meyerding family down the steps. At that moment Friedrich came bursting in through the front door, panting. Elisabeth stared at him: ' Friedrich! Why didn't you stay with Oma and Opa?'

'There wasn't any firing when I left them. I ran ever so quickly.'

'Oh, you've given me a fright. You could've been hit. Come into the cellar, quick.'

They all settled down on the makeshift benches, while Herr Meyerding lit the two candles which he kept there for these occasions.

Friedrich soon got his breath back: 'While I was

running I turned round and saw a grenade hitting the ground directly in front of the other no. 8'.

Elisabeth gasped: 'What? A grenade?'

'Yes, and some big branches of the Linden trees just outside here came down. You could see them if you went out.'

Everybody looked at Friedrich in alarm.

'You were lucky you got back here safely.' Herr Meyerding sounded very concerned.

To Elisabeth, Friedrich didn't appear all that worried. Did she detect a hint of pride in her son's voice as he related his adventure to the others? Perhaps he hadn't fully grasped the seriousness of the situation. What if he had been hit by one of those big branches coming down? She wondered about her parents, too. Hopefully they would be all right with the Kuhrau family. Probably they were all sitting in their cellar now.

While waiting anxiously, Elisabeth could hear the shooting in the distance. It seemed to go on for a long time. Anja became quite restless and turned to her mother: 'Can I go up and get my puzzle game?'

'No, you can't go up now. We have to wait here until the shooting stops.' Elisabeth looked at the others apologetically, and she was relieved when the young Frau Meyerding stepped in with the suggestion that they should all play a guessing game.

'It goes like this: I'm thinking of something which is round and red.'

'Is it an apple?' Anja was captivated immediately.

'No, it's not. But you <u>can</u> eat it.'

'It must be a tomato,' Herr Meyerding said.

'Yes, you are right, Father. Now it's your turn.'

'Well, let me think of something…'

Elisabeth could see that the old gentleman was enjoying this as much as the children were. With this entertainment they soon stopped listening out for the shooting. Even the old Frau Meyerding joined in the game, and to Elisabeth's surprise burst out laughing once or twice.

After what seemed at least two hours to Elisabeth, Herr Meyerding went up to assess the situation. But no sooner had he gone than he was back, crying out: 'Quedlinburg is on fire!' Gasping, they looked at each other in distress.

'What shall we do?' Elisabeth asked anxiously.

'Well, the shooting seems to have stopped. I think it is safe for us to go up.'

Herr Meyerding led the way. Through the open front door they could see the glow of fire in the sky over the old part of the town. Elisabeth was instantly reminded of the scene she had witnessed in Halle after the Dresden bombing. Now – even here in Quedlinburg? When would this misery end?

Herr Meyerding was confident that the shooting was over and said they should all go to bed. Elisabeth was grateful to have this kind, strong man in the house. He gave her a sense of security and she felt protected. She quickly gave the children something to eat and got them ready for bed. Tomorrow was her father's seventy-third birthday. Would they be able to sit together in the afternoon and have that cake she had made earlier in the week?

17

The War is Over

In the morning Elisabeth was woken by Friedrich's knock on the door. She jumped up: 'Oh, Friedrich, are you all right?'

'Yes, sure. But I just heard Herr Meyerding say that American soldiers are marching outside.'

'What?'

Elisabeth quickly drew the curtains, and they both stood in astonishment. A seemingly endless line of American soldiers, armed with machine guns, was passing by on the opposite side of the road.

Friedrich watched with fascination: 'They walk so quietly,' he said, 'look, they have rubber soles on their boots, not like the Germans. Their boots hit the ground so hard.'

'Yes, you're right,' Elisabeth agreed. She was puzzled about the sudden appearance of American soldiers in the town. What did this mean? Was the war over and was Quedlinburg being occupied by American forces?

She prepared a quick breakfast, and then she and the children went along to the other no. 8 to say 'Happy birthday' to Opa.

They were greeted with news of dramatic events that had taken place there in the early hours of the morning.

'What happened?' Elisabeth could see that the family, including her parents, were still in a state of agitation.

'Well,' Frau Kuhrau started to explain, 'after the gun fire had stopped last night, we stayed in the cellar. I thought it would be safer. At about 6 o'clock we heard footsteps on the stairs. We all jumped up in terror. The door was wrenched open and there stood four foreign soldiers with machine guns, just staring at us.'

'Oh no!' Elisabeth couldn't believe what she was hearing.

'Yes,' Frau Kuhrau continued, 'for a moment we froze. I noticed they were Americans. They had the letters US on their caps. Then one said in broken German: "Don't be frightened. The war is over. We are here to protect you. Now – can someone make us coffee, please?" You can imagine how relieved we were.'

'I can, indeed. Did they stay long?'

'No, not long. But they enjoyed their coffee all right. Lotte also gave them some slices of bread with jam. They were really very friendly. In the end we tried to speak a little English, and they were quite amused.'

With a sigh of relief Elisabeth turned to her father, hugging him: 'What a start to your birthday, Father!'

'Well,' he replied, 'could I have a better birthday present? The war is finally at an end.'

'You're right,' Elisabeth was still too perplexed to grasp the full meaning of what she had been told. Was it true what the American soldier had said?

'No more nights sitting in the cellar by candle light!' Frau Kuhrau called out, clapping her hands.

'It's just wonderful,' Oma exclaimed, and suddenly Elisabeth found herself on a wave of rejoicing, with the children dancing around the table, singing: 'The war is over! The war is over!'

'Happy birthday to Opa!' It was Lotte calling out, carrying in a small cake from the kitchen.

'Happy birthday!' they all repeated in loud voices.

'Oh, Lotte!' Opa looked on in surprise as Lotte put the cake on the table.

She said: 'I know you will be at Elisabeth's in the afternoon and have a bigger cake, I'm sure, but I thought we could have a little celebration now. The war is over and it's your birthday!'

'How kind of you. Thank you.'

Elisabeth could see how touched her father was by Lotte's gesture. He wiped a tear from his eyes and then started cutting the cake. As a master baker, he of all people would know what it meant to produce a cake in these circumstances, when ingredients were in such short supply.

The children didn't need much encouragement to share the unexpected treat with Opa and the rest of the family, and it wasn't long before the little cake had disappeared into very hungry mouths.

Looking at this happy scene, Elisabeth couldn't help thinking of Ludwig. Where was he at this moment? Would he be able to celebrate the end of the war in some way? If only she would hear from him soon …

In the afternoon, Elisabeth was waiting for her family to come in and spend the rest of Opa's birthday together. She had laid the table and decorated it with a small vase of spring flowers from Lotte's garden. In the middle sat her very modest version of the famous 'Streuselkuchen', a Silesian speciality, normally made with rich sugar crumble, flavoured with cinnamon. Around it she had arranged a few bread rolls filled with jam.

What a contrast to previous birthdays, when in their home town Glogau the family would assemble for the traditional 'coffee and cake' afternoon get-together. Apart from the Streuselkuchen there would be the typical Silesian poppy seed cake and a whole variety of cream gateaus, as well as Opa's popular sugar pretzels. When would they have a proper birthday celebration again, she wondered?

The children had gone round to collect their grandparents a while ago. But where were they all? She looked out of the window. There was no sign of them.

Suddenly a loud booming of guns made her start. What was that? Not shell fire again?

At that moment Friedrich came running in, calling to her: 'Mummy, come out! The Americans are firing guns in the Square.'

Elisabeth looked at him in alarm. She followed him and saw a whole crowd of people watching the spectacle in the middle of the Square. The commandant belted out the order: FIRE! All of the ten guns fired simultaneously, salvo after salvo. Elisabeth was horrified. Where were these shells flying? Why was this happening now after the soldiers had said in the morning that the war was over?

Looking across the Square, Elisabeth spotted her father. He was sitting on a high kerb, observing everything with great interest. Was he even enjoying this on his birthday?

After about fifteen minutes the commandant signalled to his men: OK. They stopped the shelling.

The crowds started to disperse and Elisabeth walked over to her father: 'You are spending a very different birthday indeed,' she said.

'Yes, I suppose so. I never thought I would watch gun firing from such short distance,' her father replied with a smile.

Elisabeth sat down beside him: 'I wonder what their target was.'

'Oh, someone said, it was the small town of Thale, about ten kilometres away from here. Obviously, they are taking town by town in this way.'

Elisabeth shook her head. She just couldn't understand what was going on.

'Oh, look!' she cried out, pointing to some soldiers who had started playing baseball.

'A minute ago they may have killed people and now they are having a jolly good time.'

'Well, that's war for you, my dear. Maybe it relieves their stress.'

Elisabeth was amazed how calm her father remained in this highly disturbing situation.

Now she saw a few soldiers handing out little silver wrapped sticks to a bunch of children. What might that be? Judging from the expression on the children's faces, they seemed to like what they were putting into their mouths, chewing away happily. Some were begging for more, and the young soldiers appeared to enjoy giving them these sweets. Elisabeth couldn't see her own children among them, though. They would be too shy .

She turned to her father: 'Your birthday coffee and cake is ready, Father. Come, let's go in.'

99

Friedrich and Anja had called for Oma who had stayed indoors. Elisabeth knew that her mother couldn't bear watching military actions. As they were walking to her home under the blossoming trees of Lindenstrasse, she was hoping that after the dramatic events of the day they would be able to spend a peaceful evening together.

18

A New Arrival

The night was quiet. There was no more gunfire, and when Elisabeth drew the curtains the next morning, her eyes were drawn to the beautiful lime trees glowing in lovely sunshine. For a moment she savoured the warm, peaceful atmosphere. The war was over. They had come through. All would be well. She was going to be hopeful.

But in a flash it came back to her what Gerda Meyerding had told her last night after her parents had gone home and the children were in bed: Thirty-five Quedlinburg residents had been killed in the shellfire they had heard while waiting anxiously in the cellar the night before. Among them was a close friend of the Meyerdings. Gerda had gone round during the day and seen the total destruction of her friend's house. What tragedy at the very end. Elisabeth remembered the shelling she herself had watched in the square. How many people had lost their lives on that occasion?

She started laying the table for breakfast, putting a piece of Streuselkuchen on both Friedrich and Anja's plates. She had saved the two pieces for them as a surprise.

And all the time she kept thinking of Ludwig. Would someone give him a piece of cake? Where was he? He had travelled east two weeks ago. What if he had fallen into Russian hands and was taken prisoner? The thought was unbearable.

At least here in Quedlinburg they were under American, not Russian, occupation and people could expect to be treated decently. Elisabeth had heard rumours of terrible acts of revenge by Russian soldiers, who were encouraged by their leaders to take advantage of German women in retaliation of what Germans had done to Russian civilians earlier in the war.

Surely, the Americans would help them build up a new life soon and especially see to it that there would be more food. Although Elisabeth's family had not gone through starvation, they had been short of about everything.

Over the following days and weeks Elisabeth noticed that the atmosphere in the town became more relaxed. People were talking to each other more openly, and the normal greeting was once again 'Guten Tag'. It felt strange at first, after being forced to say 'Heil Hitler' for so many years, but everyone got used to it quickly. Where might Hitler be, anyway? He was certainly not the 'Führer' any longer.

Elisabeth often overheard fellow refugees talking about returning to their home towns. Would her family be able to go back to Glogau, she wondered? The old Frau Meyerding would be more than happy to get rid of them. In fact, Elisabeth had heard her say so, one afternoon, when Anja came running into the house with muddy shoes.

'Now look at the mess you've made,' she had shouted at the little girl who stopped in her tracks, frightened and confused. 'You'd better all go back to where you came from. I don't want you here any longer.'

Elisabeth had immediately apologised and wiped the floor clean. But Frau Meyerding's outbreak had upset her very much. Should she look for accommodation elsewhere?

One morning, when out shopping she saw some newspapers on sale. Eagerly, she bought one, but on opening it she was startled beyond belief. There were horrific pictures of concentration camp inmates, who had recently been liberated by British forces. Back in Glogau, Elisabeth had vaguely heard of so-called labour camps. Two Jewish acquaintances had suddenly disappeared, and she had guessed that they had been transported to camps for enforced labour. She had never heard of them again.

And here she saw these awful pictures of emaciated men and women in striped prison outfits staring ahead with empty eyes. Next to them were heaps of naked corpses.

She tried to hide the papers from the children, but one day she came upon Friedrich sitting absorbed in a newspaper she had forgotten to put away. He looked up at her, stunned. Pointing to one of the pictures, he asked: 'Are these German people?'

'Yes,' Elisabeth said in a choking voice, 'I'm afraid they are.'

'But who did this to them?'

'Well, our Führer gave the order to put these people into camps and force them to work in munitions factories.'

'But why?'

'Because they were Jewish.'

Friedrich looked at her in consternation.

Elisabeth tried to explain: 'There was always talk of Hitler wanting to create a nation of pure Aryans – you know, people with blonde hair and blue eyes, like you and Anja. That was his ideal, a super nation to rule all others. And the Jews, who were darker, didn't fit in. It appears that he tried to do away with them. I really didn't know about these concentration camps.'

Elisabeth could see how disturbing all this was for Friedrich. He was a sensitive boy who cared a lot about people and was particularly protective of his little sister. It was very upsetting for her to see his distress, but she felt unable to keep this terrible news away from him. She knew he was maturing too fast and shouldn't be burdened like this. He wasn't even twelve yet. She must see to it that he went out more with his friends, especially in this lovely spring weather they were having.

She still carried on with her night duty at the hospital. The number of her patients was gradually decreasing as there were no new casualties. How happy she felt for the young soldiers, who were released one by one, healed from their injuries. She hoped they would be able to return to their loved ones and not be made prisoners of war. But what about herself? Would she be made redundant soon?

Her anxious thoughts were pushed away by a happy event on 17 May when Gerda Meyerding was delivered of a beautiful baby girl, named Ruth. As arranged, Gerda had called on Elisabeth in the morning, when she thought that the birth was imminent. The two women walked the short distance to the Maternity Clinic, arriving just in time, as little Ruth was obviously in a hurry to make her entrance into the world. All went well, and when Elisabeth visited Gerda later in the afternoon, bringing an excited Anja with her, she was relieved to see the new mother looking well and extremely happy, with her baby in a cot next to her bed.

Soon the new Quedlinburg citizen was brought home, giving her mother, her grandparents, as well as all the many friends, a lot of pleasure. Everyone wanted to see little Ruth, bringing whatever they could, a soft toy or some handed down baby clothes, or some sweets for mum. For Elisabeth it was wonderful to be allowed to assist with the baby care. It reminded her of her nursing days in a maternity ward many years ago; but to this baby she felt especially close, as she had found such a lovely friend in her mother. It was like having a third child.

However, she sensed that there remained a dark cloud hanging over this happy household. Gerda had had no news from her husband in months. Where was he? Would he ever see his daughter? Often Elisabeth could see how strained Gerda looked when she lifted her baby up, gazing at the little face with loving eyes, talking to the child, telling her how proud her daddy would be when he came home.

'Oh, Elisabeth,' she would say, ' you will understand how I feel. You miss your husband, and your children must miss their father. Where are our men? No one seems to be able to tell us.'

'Yes, you're right,' Elisabeth replied, 'I'm very worried about Ludwig. We used to be in regular contact, but it's coming up to two months now that I haven't heard anything from him.'

However, she was determined not to lose hope. Surely, he would be with them soon.

19

Fredo and Family come to Quedlinburg

One late morning when Elisabeth came home from standing in queues for vegetables and bread, Gerda was waiting for her at the entrance door.

'Don't be surprised,' she said, 'you've got a visitor.'

Elisabeth was puzzled. No sooner had she stepped into her sitting room than she stopped in her tracks. There stood her brother, smiling at her.

'Fredo!'

'Elisabeth!' He rushed towards her and took her in his arms.

'So you're free,' Elisabeth exclaimed. 'Where have you come from?'

'This minute, I've come from our parents round the corner. They told me where you were'

'Oh, Fredo, I can't believe it. When were you released?'

'Only yesterday. The French let us all go.'

Elisabeth was mystified: 'But why did you come here? Your people are in Alttöplitz.' She knew that since their escape from Silesia, Fredo's wife Liesel, and Gisela, his little daughter, as well as other members of his family had been staying in a holiday cottage belonging to a relative. It was just outside Berlin, in a small town which was now in the Russian occupied zone.

'Yes, and I want to get them away from there as soon as I can. They are living in constant fear of Russian soldiers. Liesel is particularly worried about Gretel.'

'Oh, of course, I understand.' Elisabeth looked at her brother with concern. Gretel was Liesel's younger sister. She was a very attractive blonde girl of only seventeen. No wonder they feared for her safety in this situation.

'Liesel said in her letter that they run and hide in nearby woods whenever they hear a military vehicle approaching. It's revolting.'

Elisabeth could sense how upset her brother was about it all.

'Oh, Fredo, how horrible. So do you want to bring them here?'

'Yes, I'd like that very much. Our parents have just introduced me to Frau Kuhrau. She said she might be able to find somewhere for us to stay.'

Elisabeth was not surprised: 'I'm sure Frau Kuhrau will help. She has a lot of contacts in the town. Oh, it'll be lovely to have you all here.' She patted him on his shoulder. 'I do wish you luck.'

'Thank you. I'll let you know how I get on. I just wanted to say hello quickly'.

'It's so good to see you, Fredo. You're looking well '

'That's nice to hear, Sis. Now I'd better press on. Take care.'

He quickly took his leave, and Elisabeth started unpacking her meagre shopping bag. She felt quite dazed. Her brother Fredo was here! In fact, she hadn't told the truth when she said he was looking well. She thought he had lost a lot of weight and his face was drawn.

The last time they had seen each other he was in his military uniform. He had been a professional soldier and had risen to the rank of major. Elisabeth had heard him say long ago how futile this war was. Having experienced the slaughter of Stalingrad in 1942 he obviously knew that Germany would never win. How right he had been.

Elisabeth remembered the day when the news of his terrible injury came through. He had been shot in the stomach. The family were devastated and feared for his life. Miraculously, he pulled through and recovered well. Liesel had told Elisabeth about her daily visits to the military hospital in their home town Breslau. She'd hoped that Fredo would be spared further service. However, as soon as he was well enough, he had been sent back to the front, this time in the West rather than the East. So, at the end he had become a prisoner of war in the French occupied zone of Germany and been released early.

How she wished that Ludwig was here, too. It was now almost two months that he had left them after his short visit in April. Where might he be?

Within a week Fredo's family arrived in Quedlinburg. Frau Kuhrau had found a place for them in the house of the Catholic priest. She told Elisabeth that she had known Father Peter from her days at the Music College in Halberstadt, where he had given a short lecture series on hymnology. Although she herself was not a Catholic, she had always remained in contact with him. And it seemed only natural to turn to him for help on this occasion.

Elisabeth was curious to know how her brother's family would get on in such a religious environment. Would they start going to church now?

She soon went to pay them a visit. When she rang the bell at the big presbytery, opposite the Catholic Church, a portly lady came to open the door. She had a sceptical look on her face.

'Oh, hello,' Elisabeth tried to be as friendly as she could. 'I would like to see my brother and his family. They came here a few days ago. Their name is Fellmann.'

'Ah, I know. Come in.'

The lady, who Elisabeth presumed to be the priest's housekeeper, led the way up a wide staircase to the first floor. She pointed to a door along the landing: 'That's were they are.'

'Thank you very much.' Elisabeth went and knocked on the door.

There was great excitement, as she was greeted warmly by the four female members of the Fellmann family. Her brother Fredo was out.

'Sit down, I'll make a cup of coffee,' Liesel exclaimed. She seemed thrilled to see Elisabeth. 'I'll just get some fresh water.'

'Oh lovely, thank you, Liesel.' Elisabeth watched her as she took a saucepan from a wooden shelf and left the room. Elisabeth looked at the others, puzzled.

'We have to get the water from the kitchen downstairs.' Gretel explained.

'Really?' Elisabeth was very surprised. 'Isn't there a tap up here, in the bathroom perhaps?'

'Yes, but we're not allowed to use that.'

Oma Lasswitz, Liesel's mother, joined in the conversation now: 'We have to do the cooking in here, as well.' She pointed to a corner of the room: 'That's our cooker, just a hob with two gas burners.'

Elisabeth couldn't believe what she was hearing: 'But some of you sleep in here. I can see two beds. Wouldn't it be dangerous, in case there was a gas leak?'

'Oh yes, this is where Fredo and Liesel sleep. Gretel, Gisela and I sleep in the other room.'

Gisela was keen to show it to her aunt. She took Elisabeth's hand and said:' Come with me, Auntie Elisabeth.' She opened the door to an adjacent room. Elisabeth was amazed to see how cramped it looked. There was hardly any space between the three beds. A small wardrobe was squeezed into one corner.

'Is this all you have?' Elisabeth asked, stepping back into the main room.

'Yes,' Oma Lasswitz replied in a rather sad tone of voice.

'But this house is very large. Couldn't they have let you have another room for the five of you?'

'Well,' Gretel went on, 'there are quite a lot of people living here. We haven't spoken to them yet. They seem to be refugees, too.'

'Oh, I see, that may be the reason.' Elisabeth wondered if it was on Frau Kuhrau's recommendation that Father Peter had agreed to take this family in, as well, when the house was almost fully occupied.

In the meantime, Liesel was back with fresh water and started to make coffee.

'Where is Fredo?' Elisabeth asked.

'He's gone to an office to find out about jobs. He was also going to enquire about a teachers' training course. He said he would quite like to train as a teacher.'

'That would be nice.' Elisabeth had always thought that her brother would make a good teacher. 'He would certainly keep good discipline in the classroom.'

'Oh yes,' Liesel laughed. 'The kids wouldn't play an ex-soldier up, that's for sure.'

'Are you looking for a job, as well?' Elisabeth asked.

'Yes, I'd like to go in for dressmaking,' Liesel said.

'Oh, wonderful. You've always been good at that, Liesel.' Elisabeth envied her sister-in-law's talent, as she herself had never been good at sewing. Especially in these dire times it would be so useful to be able to make your own clothes, particularly for the children.

'Well, I'd better be on my way,' Elisabeth said after enjoying her coffee. 'I'm so glad you're here. I hope you come and see us soon.'

'Yes.' Liesel said, 'and we'll also go and visit Oma and Opa Fellmann.'

On her way home Elisabeth kept thinking how happy her parents must be to have their son's family living near them now, as well. Although they were at the other end of the town they would surely see each other as often as possible.

20

The Russians take over in Quedlinburg

Over the next few weeks rumours regarding the occupying forces created growing anxiety among the people of Quedlinburg.

While queuing for vegetables one morning, Elisabeth heard a man say: 'I can't see many American soldiers in the streets anymore. Are they getting ready to leave?'

'Oh, yes,' a woman replied. 'The Russians are on their way, for sure. It happened in my cousin's town, Bernburg, not far from here. She told me in a letter today that three nights ago the Americans left, and the Russians were there the next morning.'

Elisabeth was horrified to hear this and looked at the woman in disbelief. The Russians, with their terrible reputation, were coming here? She felt quite dazed, and quickly went to share her news with Gerda, on her return. She, too, had heard similar reports.

Elisabeth felt devastated. 'Oh, Gerda, what are we going to do? How are we going to protect ourselves and our children, if the rumours about the Russian soldiers are true?'

There was a gurgling noise from the cot in the corner that made the two women look up and smile. Little Ruth was wanting to have her say. Gerda picked her up. She looked so beautiful and her sweet smile let Elisabeth forget her dark thoughts for a moment.

But the anxiety about what might happen remained with her day and night. Often she couldn't fall asleep for a long time and she regularly woke up early.

It was on the first of July that the rumour finally turned into fact: The Russians had arrived in Quedlinburg overnight. Friedrich was the first to know. It was his duty to fetch the milk for the families at Lindenstrasse 8 each morning. Normally, Elisabeth could hear his cheerful whistle when he came back. But this morning, he appeared quite agitated.

'What's the matter?' she asked him.

He told her: 'When I got to Reichenstrasse I noticed small red posters pinned to several house doors and gates. I stopped and read one. It said in big print at the top: WE WELCOME THE VICTORIOUS RUSSIAN ARMY. There were a few small lines in the middle, and at the bottom it said: COMMUNISTIC PARTY OF GERMANY.'

Elisabeth was stunned. So it was true. The Russians were here. It meant they were now living in a kind of prison. She had heard that people were not allowed to travel freely under Russian occupation. If only she had news from Ludwig. Where was he? Perhaps even in Russian captivity? Was he still alive? Gerda hadn't heard from her husband either. Were the two of them going to be war widows?

She gave a strong warning to Friedrich, who was fond of strolling through the streets with his friends: 'Don't ever go near a Russian soldier! They can't be trusted. They are not like the Americans, who are our friends. Do you hear?'

'Yes.' Friedrich looked at her, quite shocked. The

children of the neighbourhood had become very friendly with some of the patrolling American soldiers, and once or twice Friedrich had come in with sticks of chewing gum to share with Anja.

But Russians? No! Elisabeth was most concerned that he should keep his distance. She hoped she would not have to face any of them herself.

However, it wasn't long before Friedrich came home one afternoon, telling her excitedly that he and his friend Bernd had watched a group of Russian soldiers in the street.

'One was playing a mouth organ, and three were dancing.'

Elisabeth stared at him, aghast: 'What? Dancing in the street?'

'Yes, look – like this,' Friedrich tried to demonstrate their steps to her. 'They were holding on to each other, stamping their feet very hard on the ground, to the music, and then, almost squatting, threw their feet about – very fast. It was really good.'

'Oh, Friedrich! Where was that?'

'In Steinweg.'

'That's not very far from here.'

'There were lots of people there. They all clapped. And then the soldiers asked two boys to join them and taught them the dance. And afterwards they gave some children sweets.'

Elisabeth couldn't believe what she was hearing.

'But you didn't accept sweets, did you?'

'No, of course not. Bernd and I went away quickly. He wanted me to go home with him for a bit, to play with his trains.'

Elisabeth didn't know what to make of it all. Russian soldiers dancing in the street, handing out sweets to children… Maybe it was their way of worming themselves into the children's families, and then the women would have to pay the price? She felt a shudder going through her.

The awful uncertainty made coping with everyday life very hard indeed. Elisabeth was still working at the hospital, and was grateful for the income, albeit small. Much of her time was taken up with finding food for her family. Provisions were not as good as she had hoped, and with the Russians in charge, it wasn't going to get any better.

She wondered how her brother and his family were getting on. She hadn't heard from them for a while. She must go and see them soon. They had been so happy to have managed to come to the American Zone. What a disappointment this must be for them. At least they had found good accommodation in the Catholic priest's house.

But there were also some pleasant surprises in these anxious times. One afternoon Elisabeth's father knocked on her door with a broad smile on his face, holding something behind his back.

'Hello, everyone!' he said.

Anja came running along as soon as she heard Opa's voice: 'What are you hiding behind your back?' she asked, trying to see.

'You have to smell it – and then you'll know,' he said, showing them a big bulging paper bag. Both Elisabeth and Anja eagerly put their noses to the bag.

'Oh, Opa.' Elisabeth knew instantly what is was. He opened the bag.

'A loaf of bread! Where did you get that? It smells so fresh.'

'I made it myself!'

'How? Not in Frau Kuhrau's kitchen?'

'No. I made it in a real bakery.'

'You didn't! Do tell us. What have you been up to?'

They sat down in Elisabeth's living room and Opa told them how the other day he had wandered into a bakery, just along the road, asking whether they needed any assistance. As it happened they did, and so he had started his new job.

Elisabeth was amazed: 'You are full of surprises, dear Father.'

'Well, it's only a few hours each day. It keeps me out of Oma's way, and it's lovely to work in my own trade. They are very nice people, and today they offered me this extra loaf. I thought you should have it.'

'It smells wonderful, Opa, and it looks so shiny.' Anja couldn't keep her hands off it. 'Can we have some now, Mummy, with jam?'

'Yes, of course, and I'll make a cup of coffee for Opa.'

While she was preparing the unexpected little afternoon treat, Elisabeth couldn't help feeling great pride in her father. He certainly had guts, and she was determined to follow his example and not let the difficulties of the present time get her down.

21

Summer Activities and a Wonderful Event

School and Kindergarten were closed for the summer, but there was no shortage of activities to keep the children occupied.

Anja often went to play with Ingrid at the other no. 8. That house with its open and friendly atmosphere had become a little haven for many children and Elisabeth couldn't be more grateful that Friedrich and Anja were part of it.

Sometimes Gisela, Elisabeth's little niece, would join them there when she came over with her parents. In Silesia they had lived in different towns, and it was nice for Elisabeth to see how well the two six-year old cousins got on with each other.

Gisela was obviously also making herself useful at the Presbytery. One day when Elisabeth met her at her grandparents', playing Snakes and Ladders together, she told them: 'I feed the hens in the backyard. I collect lots of cockchafers. The hens like them. And then Frau Bölte gives me an egg.'

Elisabeth was amused. Here was a little business woman growing up. She couldn't see her own daughter doing something like that.

Anja also spent a lot of time with baby Ruth whom she looked upon as her own little sister. No sooner had she spotted Gerda taking the baby into the garden than she ran out to talk to her. The old Frau Meyerding still didn't like Anja to be there. Indeed, Elisabeth had observed her looking at the little girl suspiciously, but refraining from saying anything in front of her daughter-in-law.

For Elisabeth it was lovely to watch Anja happily helping Gerda with some gardening. She paid close attention to Gerda when she explained to her about various flowers, and she was very keen when it came to picking fruit. Elisabeth noticed that Gerda made sure that her mother-in-law was out of sight when she gave Anja her reward for helping – a small tub of berries to share with her mother and brother.

Opa was carrying on with his job at the bakery. His work was obviously very much appreciated, as every week he brought an extra loaf of bread for the family and sometimes even a much valued pound or two of flour. Elisabeth and Gerda would then join together for a baking session in the kitchen, and soon a cake, topped with the fruit from the garden, would be shared by all the family at Lindenstrasse 8. Old Frau Meyerding certainly didn't complain about that.

For Friedrich life was getting quite exciting. All school children of his age were called by the town council to carry out a type of 'field service' during the summer holidays. As Elisabeth was told, there were huge turnip and sugar beet fields outside the town, and the children were asked to do weeding and thinning out of plants.

Each morning she saw Friedrich off at 7 o'clock. In his little shoulder bag he carried a bottle of water and a sandwich to have with the cup of soup he would be given at their lunch break. The children assembled on the big square Kleers and were driven out on lorries. Elisabeth could see how much Friedrich looked forward to these drives, when he would meet his friends. They were obviously having great fun, talking and telling jokes.

Like other mothers she was apprehensive at first. Where exactly were they taking the children? What if they didn't bring them back? But as time went by and Friedrich came home safe and sound each afternoon, she stopped worrying. She was happy for him to be occupied in this way. The fresh air was doing him good and she was pleased to see him looking tanned and contented on his return.

Quedlinburg – Nikolai church

On Sundays he usually went to church with his grandparents and he seemed to enjoy that. Elisabeth wondered how much he would understand of the sermon. The elderly pastor and the whole atmosphere at the church appeared to make a deep impression on him.

One Sunday he told her that the service had been taken by a different pastor: 'He is called Mr Zaremba and he comes from Silesia, too. He is going to start a Bible Story afternoon on Tuesdays, for refugee children.'

'How nice.' Elisabeth could sense Friedrich's enthusiasm. 'Would you like to go?'

'Yes, I would. Perhaps Bernd can come, too. But he is not a refugee.'

'Oh, I'm sure Mr Zaremba will let him come with you,' Elisabeth said encouragingly, 'you go and tell Bernd.'

And so it happened that their Tuesday evening meals became their 'story time'. It was long ago that in her own Sunday school days Elisabeth had heard about Moses, the Judges and the first Kings of Israel, Saul and David, and she was as eager as Anja to listen to Friedrich telling them what he had heard earlier in the afternoon. He impressed her with his good memory and his ability to bring the stories to life for them.

Elisabeth was amazed at how much confidence and resilience her children had developed during these summer weeks. Despite their frugal diet they appeared to be very healthy.

They were out and about most of the time in the hot weather, enjoying the long days with their friends. And she felt happy for them.

However, there was one nagging thought that wouldn't leave her: Where was Ludwig? Why hadn't she heard from him? When he left them in April he had boarded a train heading east. Had he fallen into Russian hands? There were rumours that German prisoners of war had been transported to Russia. Was Ludwig among them?

She sensed that Gerda was burdened in the same way. She hadn't heard from her husband Hans for almost a year.

The two women sometimes sat together in the garden talking while watching over baby Ruth. One Sunday afternoon Gerda appeared to be lost in thought. Suddenly she said in a low voice: 'You know, I think Hans is dead,' and tears started trickling down her face.

Elisabeth was shocked to see her friend in such distress. It was only the baby crying at that moment which kept Gerda from breaking down completely. Elisabeth lifted little Ruth out of her pram and put her into her mother's arms. She said: 'I know how you feel, Gerda. But we must not lose hope. Some men have already returned home. Why shouldn't it be Hans next?'

'Yes, you're right,' Gerda replied with a deep sigh, looking lovingly at her baby, 'I suppose we have to go on hoping.'

The next day, Monday 20 August, Elisabeth was sitting in her room in the evening, reading, after the children had gone to bed. Suddenly she was startled by a loud knock on the front door. She froze in her chair. Who might that be? Not the Secret Police searching for Nazis hiding in friends' houses? What should she do? The old couple had retired early, as usual, and would be asleep by now. Gerda on the second floor might not have heard the knocking.

Carefully Elisabeth opened her door and tiptoed out into the hall. Another knock made her jump.

'Anybody in?' someone called.

At that moment Gerda came rushing down the stairs. The two women looked at each other, holding their breath.

Another knock.

Gerda called out: 'Who is it?'

'It's me, Hans.'

With a suppressed scream, Gerda turned the key with trembling hands and opened the door. A tall, skeletal figure stood motionless before them. He was leaning against the door frame as if he needed its support to hold himself up.

'Hans!' Gerda cried out in a choking voice. She flung her arms around her husband: 'Darling, you're back. Come inside.'

For a moment, Elisabeth looked on, stunned. Then she quickly went back into her room, while Gerda led her husband upstairs.

She sat down, feeling quite numb with emotion. How wonderful this was for Gerda. She couldn't but be happy for her.

Would there be another knock on the door one day? And would it be Ludwig?

22

Planning new Arrangements

When Elisabeth told the children the next morning that Gerda's husband had come home, Friedrich asked immediately: 'Will Father be back, as well, now?'

'Oh, I do hope so. They must let the prisoners of war go home soon.'

She tried not to let the children see how anxious she was, but the waiting got harder by the day. Why hadn't Ludwig written for so long? Would they ever see him again? What would happen to them if he didn't come back?

Last night's incident was still vivid in her mind. Even now she could imagine how worried Gerda was about her husband. She must have been as shocked as Elisabeth was when she saw him standing at the door, his clothes just hanging on him and his face emaciated. What terrible times of starvation must he have endured? Was this the way prisoners of war were treated by the Russians? Would Ludwig look like this when he came home?

Later in the day Gerda told Elisabeth that Hans was seriously ill. He had slipped in and out of consciousness during the night, talking in his sleep, and when he tried to get up in the morning he had collapsed on the floor. She could hardly get him back into bed. This commotion had frightened the baby who had started crying and whining pitifully. The doctor had been in to see Hans and ordered strict rest for at least two weeks.

'I'm devastated to hear this,' Elisabeth said, 'can I help in any way?'

'Well,' Gerda hesitated before she went on: 'I hate to say this, Elisabeth. But seeing Hans in this state, I really think we will need your rooms now, as they are on the ground floor. I'm so sorry. I'll be very sad to lose you.'

'Oh, don't worry, Gerda. I understand.' Gerda's words had quite thrown her, but Elisabeth tried not to show her disappointment of having to leave Lindenstrasse 8. 'You've got to think of your family first. I'm sure I'll be able to find somewhere else soon.'

'I'll help you, of course,' Gerda said reassuringly, 'maybe we can find a place for you not far from here. Then we'll still be able to see each other quite often.'

'That would be lovely.' Elisabeth patted Gerda's shoulder. 'But you must see to your husband now and help him to recover.'

She felt so close to Gerda and would miss their conversations very much. She knew that a move would be quite unsettling for the three of them. Where would they go? Anja was so fond of little Ruth, and Friedrich had been such help to Gerda getting the milk for the baby each morning.

But at least they wouldn't have to face old Frau Meyerding's rude and hostile behaviour in future. Especially now that her son had returned home, she wouldn't want strangers in her house any longer. Surely, things would turn out all right in the end.

The same afternoon, Elisabeth went to share her problem with her friends at the other no. 8. She found Frau

Kuhrau and her daughter Lotte sitting in the kitchen having a cup of coffee together.

As soon as she had explained the situation, the ever resourceful Frau Kuhrau sprang into action, saying: 'Perhaps we can do a swap. I know a retired couple, Herr and Frau Russwurm. They live in Julius-Wolff-Strasse, a stone's throw away from here. They have a big house. I heard the other day they would be willing to take people in, preferably older ones. So if your parents went there, you could come here with Friedrich and Anja. How about that?'

Elisabeth was stunned: 'Frau Kuhrau, that would be lovely. Are you sure?'

'Yes – unless they've already got someone else. Of course, here you would only have the one room on the top floor where your parents are.'

'I know. But we'd manage. It's a nice big room.'

However, Elisabeth couldn't help feeling uneasy about this whole matter. Should she expect her parents to agree to yet another upheaval?

Frau Kuhrau was getting quite excited: 'I tell you what. I'll pop over there later and enquire.'

While they were still talking Opa returned from the bakery. Elisabeth could see his surprise at finding her in the Kuhrau kitchen: 'Is everything all right at Lindenstrasse 8?' he asked.

'Well, yes and no,' Elisabeth replied. 'There was great excitement for Gerda. Her husband Hans has returned home.'

'That's wonderful.' Opa sat down while Lotte poured him a cup of coffee.

'Yes,' Elisabeth continued, telling him about her

conversation with Gerda earlier in the day, 'but it means we have to leave.'

'I see. And where will you go?' Opa sounded concerned.

Elisabeth looked across to Frau Kuhrau, who explained everything to him.

'Would you mind moving very much?' Elisabeth asked her father.

'No, not at all and I'm sure Oma won't either. Where is this place?'

'In Julius-Wolff-Strasse, with Herr and Frau Russwurm.'

'Oh, I know Frau Russwurm. She comes to the bakery every week. She is a nice lady. I've spoken to her several times. We'll be fine in her house, I'm sure.'

By now Oma had joined them. She agreed straight away to the plan, if it would help Elisabeth and the children. She said: 'Friedrich and Anja seem to almost live here, anyway, and Bernd and Ingrid will love it.'

'It's going to be very lively,' Lotte gave Elisabeth an intriguing smile, 'we'll have to put strict house rules down, I suppose.'

'Yes, certainly,' Elisabeth nodded, smiling back at Lotte, 'we mustn't let things get out of hand.'

Elisabeth could sense Frau Kuhrau's enthusiasm, and before they knew it she was on her way, waving to them: 'Just wait here. I won't be long.' she called.

And, indeed, it was hardly half an hour later that she returned from her little mission. Elisabeth wondered what she would have to say to them:

'Well, Herr and Frau Russwurm send their regards. They look forward to meeting Herr and Frau Fellmann tomorrow morning. They appeared a little reluctant at first. But I think that's only natural. They are quite elderly. I bet once they've met our Oma and Opa Fellmann they won't have any reservations.'

'I'm sure they won't.' Lotte turned to Oma and Opa: 'Our loss is their gain. We'll miss you very much, but I guess you'll be more comfortable there. I've never been in their house. It looks big to me.'

'It certainly is,' Frau Kuhrau sounded impressed, 'there are two storeys above the ground floor. I expect they'll let you have more than one room.'

'That would be lovely,' was Oma's response. She seemed happy enough about the proposed change. Elisabeth guessed she just wanted the best for the rest of them.

'Whatever it'll be, we'll be fine, won't we?' she said to her husband.

'Of course, we will.' Opa agreed.

Elisabeth could hardly believe how speedily things were developing. It wasn't even twenty-four hours ago that Gerda's husband had knocked on the front door. She felt very relieved and said to Frau Kuhrau: 'I can't thank you enough for helping us again.'

'Oh, it's a great pleasure,' Frau Kuhrau replied, 'I'm sure we'll get on fine together. We do know each other quite well by now, don't we?'

For once Elisabeth couldn't get away quickly enough. Gerda would be so pleased to hear about these arrangements. It meant that the two of them could stay in close contact and Elisabeth would be able to continue to assist with the baby care, especially now that Gerda had the extra burden of looking after her sick husband.

23

Visit to Julius-Wolff-Strasse

The next morning Elisabeth accompanied her parents to Julius-Wolff-Strasse 3, to meet Herr and Frau Russwurm.

She felt quite apprehensive as they walked towards the house across a wide, tree-lined green. Was it going to be the right place for her parents? They were so happy living with the family at the other no. 8. Would they get on with the Russwurms whom Frau Kuhrau had described as quite elderly and somewhat reluctant when first asked about the accommodation?

Her parents seemed to take it all in such good spirits. It was just as well that Frau Russwurm was a customer at the bakery where her father had met her.

The house looked delightful with its large windows. When they rang the bell, the immaculate oak front door was opened by a tall, white-haired gentleman. He smiled at them, and although he appeared reserved Elisabeth sensed warmth in his voice when he greeted them: 'Good day to you. You must be Herr and Frau Fellmann. I am Herr Russwurm. Please, come in.'

'Thank you,' Elisabeth's father said, 'we have brought our daughter with us, as well.'

'Aha, pleased to meet you.'

They all shook hands and Herr Russwurm led the way through a wide hall into a large sitting room, where Frau Russwurm was waiting to meet them.

Elisabeth was curious to see how the lady of the house would react when she saw her father.

'Hello!' Frau Russwurm exclaimed, 'So you are Herr Fellmann! We've met in the bakery!'

'Yes,' Elisabeth's father replied, 'and who would have thought I'd come and ask to live in your house?'

'Well, I never!' Frau Russwurm gave a big smile and Elisabeth sensed that she was pleased, if taken aback. She turned to her husband: 'Arthur, I have known Herr Fellmann for quite a while. We've chatted in the bakery.'

Elisabeth could see the surprise in Herr Russwurm's face, when he answered: 'How astonishing. I remember now that you talked about someone in the bakery.' With a twinkle in his eye he added, 'I was wondering who that might be?'

This remark made them all laugh and immediately broke the ice. Elisabeth felt great relief. Things might turn out well after all.

Herr and Frau Russwurm appeared to show genuine interest in her parents – asking questions about their escape from Silesia and the long, arduous journey to Quedlinburg.

'You must miss your home very much.' Frau Russwurm was shaking her head as she looked at Elisabeth and her parents.

'Yes, we do,' her mother replied, 'but we have been made to feel at home here by many people. And that's a great comfort.'

'Well, we hope you will feel at home in our house.' Herr Russwurm said. 'We thought we would let you have two rooms on the second floor. There is a nice roof garden for you to sit out on.'

'Oh, my parents will love that.' Elisabeth exclaimed, smiling at them.

Frau Russwurm seemed eager to get things moving: 'Come, I'll show you,' she beckoned, leading the way upstairs.

Elisabeth had noticed how impeccably clean and tidy the sitting room was kept. Going up the highly polished wooden staircase, she wondered who was doing the housework. Surely not the Russwurms themselves? She judged them to be quite a bit older than her parents. Probably they employed someone; or would they expect her parents to do the cleaning?

On the first floor landing she spotted a framed board on the wall, with calligraphic lettering. It said: 'House Rules'. What might this mean? There was an identical board on the second floor. It was signed with: Dr A. Russwurm, retired mining engineer. How intriguing. Passing by quickly, as she followed the others, she wasn't able to decipher any details. Her parents didn't seem to have noticed the boards, and as Frau Russwurm didn't point them out, Elisabeth pretended not to have seen them. She couldn't help smiling to herself, though. House Rules – for her parents?

She was pleasantly surprised when she saw the rooms that were to be their home from now on. Sunlight was flooding through the large windows, creating a warm and cosy atmosphere. There was certainly enough space for her parents' few belongings. Elisabeth envied them the large wardrobe. She could do with that for herself and the children.

'This is wonderful,' her mother called out as she looked around.

Frau Russwurm smiled: 'Well, I hope you will be comfortable here.'

Opening a French window she added: 'And this is the roof garden.'

'Oh, what a lovely view we have from up here!' Elisabeth's father exclaimed. She could see how impressed he was as he looked down onto the green.

While her parents stepped out, Elisabeth turned to Frau Russwurm: 'Thank you very much. I'm more than pleased that my parents will be able to live in your house, especially as it's just round the corner from us. My children will be happy to see their grandparents quite often. They are all very fond of each other.'

'That's good to hear. So I hope everything will turn out all right.'

'I see that you have house rules.' Elisabeth couldn't resist mentioning her observation.

'Oh yes. Actually, my husband is very strict about this. We do like to have certain things done our way, for example, switching the lights off on the landing, and not turning water taps on after 10 o'clock at night. The rules are there to remind everybody.'

'Aha. I understand.' Elisabeth still felt intrigued about this.

'We'll explain everything to your parents when they come.' Frau Russwurm concluded with a smile.

During the little tour of the house, Herr Russwurm had stayed downstairs. Now he came out of his study to say goodbye. Through the open door Elisabeth could see tall bookshelves covering a whole wall of the room. On the big desk in front of a large window lay numerous open books. This was certainly a studious gentleman.

She wondered whether he would ever have time for a chat. Her father enjoyed talking to people and had the knack of drawing them out. Would he succeed with a Doctor of Mining Engineering, though?

'So we expect you tomorrow then?' Herr Russwurm said while shaking hands again with everyone.

'Yes, if that's all right with you.' Elisabeth's father replied.

Frau Russwurm patted Elisabeth's mother on the shoulder, saying: 'We can discuss the kitchen arrangements when you come, all right?'

Elisabeth was glad that her mother's 'thank you' sounded really happy.

As they walked back across the green, she could sense that her parents were looking forward to moving into their new abode. It was certainly a lovely place, and the Russwurms' kind, if reserved manner showed that they had taken to her parents. She wouldn't have to worry about them.

24

Move to Brechtstrasse 8 – A Postcard arrives

A few days after the grandparents had moved out of the other no. 8, Elisabeth and the children moved in. Both Friedrich and Anja were most excited about living in their friends' house. From now on the house in Lindenstrasse would be called the other no. 8. They knew they were still welcome there, especially with Gerda and baby Ruth, but they weren't going to miss the old Frau Meyerding, who had so often made life difficult for them. When Elisabeth went to say Goodbye to her on their last day, she gave her a devious look, mumbling something inaudible, and just walked away.

Frau Kuhrau and her daughter Lotte had worked very hard on the big room at the top of the house, rearranging the furniture and giving it a good clean. When they were carrying boxes and suitcases up, Elisabeth noticed a wardrobe outside the room on the landing that hadn't been there before.

'It's for you,' Lotte pointed out. 'I thought you'd probably need some extra space.'

'Lotte, how kind of you.' Elisabeth was very touched. 'I'm really grateful. We do seem to have collected quite a lot of things over the summer months.'

'I'm sure we can move another chest of drawers up here, too.' Lotte said.

'Oh, thank you.' Elisabeth hardly knew what to say.

While she was busy putting their clothes and other belongings into the cupboards and drawers, Anja kept looking out of the window, down onto the street, watching people pass by.

'This is how it was in Glogau, isn't it?' Elisabeth heard her call out suddenly.

She was taken aback by Anja's remark: 'You're right. Can you remember our flat there?'

'Yes, but I always had to stand on my little stool when I wanted to look out, didn't I?'

'You did. Now you don't need that. It shows how much you've grown!'

It was strange being reminded of her home town. In her hectic day-to-day life here, Elisabeth hadn't given it much thought lately.

'Are we going back to Glogau soon, Mummy?' Anja turned to her mother.

'I really can't tell you, darling.'

Anja's question made Elisabeth feel rather uneasy. She went over to her stroking her hair as they looked out across the big square together. Suddenly they spotted a little figure in the distance skipping towards their house.

'That's Ingrid!' Anja cried out. In a flash she was gone, running downstairs to greet her friend.

Elisabeth was relieved not to have to continue with this conversation. She knew there was no way they would ever return to Glogau. The town lay in ruins and the whole region of Silesia now belonged to Poland. Perhaps the Poles had started clearing the rubble?

She stepped back from the window and looked around in the big room. Lotte and her mother had really done their best to make it homely for them. She couldn't but be grateful to have these kind friends. She felt safe here, and it was surely wonderful that Friedrich and Anja were so much part of this family already.

But what of the future? Day in and day out she was wondering what had happened to Ludwig. When would she hear from him? What should she do if he didn't come back? Her financial situation was getting more difficult by the week. She had been told that her night duty in the hospital would finish at the end of September. That gave her barely four weeks to find another job. Her parents had said they would be able to help out, but she didn't want to rely on them.

She was just looking into their food basket to see what she could find for their evening meal, when she heard someone rushing up the stairs. A knock on the door made her jump.

'Come in. – Gerda! What's the matter? Is anything wrong?'

'No.' Gerda smiled at her. She was holding something in her hand. 'But there may be good news for you. The postman has just delivered this to our house. He didn't know you had moved.'

She handed Elisabeth a postcard. Elisabeth stared at it: Ludwig's handwriting! Clutching the card with trembling fingers, she glanced over the words: *I'm in Eschwege with Father. Everything is fine. Hope you and the children are well. Keep counting the sheep. Love to all. L.*

She looked at Gerda: 'I can't believe it. Ludwig is in West Germany – with his father.'

'Elisabeth, that's wonderful!' Gerda rushed up to her friend and hugged her.

Elisabeth read the card out loud. Gerda was puzzled about the *counting of the sheep*.

'Oh, that's a secret code we arranged between us when Ludwig was here on his last visit in April. It means he's trying to get here.'

'He doesn't say when, though.' Gerda gave Elisabeth a concerned look.

'No, that might be too dangerous to write,' Elisabeth explained. 'But I really don't know how he will manage to get across the border. I hear it is heavily guarded by Russian soldiers.'

'Yes, I have read about that, too.' Gerda agreed

Elisabeth looked at the card closely: 'The post stamp is the 20 August. Today is the 3 September. It's taken two weeks to get here.'

'A long time, but it proves the postal service is working.'

'Yes, thank God for that. But there is no sender address for me to reply to. I can't tell him we've moved.'

'I see. Maybe he is already on his way? Oh, Elisabeth, you'll leave us for good soon, won't you?' Now Gerda's voice sounded sad.

Elisabeth looked at her friend woefully: 'I suppose so.'

She was in a rather confused state. A few minutes ago she thought she was settling into a new home, and now it looked as if she would be on the move again in the near future.

'But I'm very happy for you.' Gerda said. 'At last your family will be together after all this time. I know what it feels like.'

136

'Yes, you're right. It will be wonderful.' Elisabeth put the card on the table. Was it really true that Ludwig had written?

Turning to Gerda she asked: 'Is Hans feeling a bit better now?'

'Yes, I think so, but it will be a long time before he's fully recovered. He's so happy to see his little daughter. He's started playing with her, and they're getting to know each other gradually'.

'That's lovely. I must come round soon and see Ruth again. Otherwise she won't know me anymore.'

'You do that, Elisabeth. But now you'd better enjoy your wonderful news.'

With that Gerda quickly left.

Elisabeth was still stunned. She read the postcard over and over again. Ludwig – in West Germany! Would he be able to come soon and get them all across that dreaded border to start a new life in the West? She hardly dared hope.

25

Looking forward to the new School Year

Elisabeth would have loved to tell the children that their father had sent a postcard and might be with them soon, but she knew she had to keep her news to herself for the time being. In their excitement they might easily tell their friends about it, and they in turn would tell their parents. Who knows, word might get round to someone connected with the Russian Secret Police. There were rumours that they were taking former German soldiers from their homes in the middle of the night. Wasn't there that family who had been left in complete ignorance as to the whereabouts of their soldier son? Newspaper reports talked of transportations to Siberian labour camps.

What if Ludwig on his journey here had fallen into the hands of the Russian Police and been interrogated? After all, he had served under Hitler. That he had been forced into it would count for nothing now. She didn't dare think about what might happen. If only she could get in touch with him.

She was certain that Gerda wouldn't talk about this recent development, and when she told Frau Kuhrau and Lotte about Ludwig's postcard and that they might see a tall man standing in front of their door one day soon, they too, promised not to breathe a word to anyone.

Her parents appeared to be delighted when they heard her news, although she could sense their sadness about losing her and the children soon.

As always, her father was trying to be encouraging: 'It will be wonderful for you, once you've made it across that wretched border.'

'Yes, I suppose so,' Elisabeth replied, 'and as soon as we are settled you must come, too.'

'Oh, don't worry about us. We are happy here now,' her mother said. But Elisabeth knew she was trying to hide her true feelings.

'You seem to have settled in well.' Elisabeth looked around the room. 'It feels very comfortable. And you certainly have more space now.'

They told her how amused they were about the 'house rules' which Herr Russwurm had read out to them quite ceremoniously on their first evening. They had given their word to follow them to the letter and to instruct their grandchildren accordingly when they came to visit. They must wipe their shoes on the doormat inside the front door and not make any noise while going upstairs.

'But I think the Russwurms will be quite easy to get on with.' Elisabeth's mother sounded very confident. 'The kitchen sharing is going to work out all right. I can cook our lunch early, as Opa has to be at the bakery by 1 o'clock. The Russwurms only have a light lunch and do their cooking in the evening.'

Her father said he had noticed that the Russwurms went to bed late, and got up late as well, and that Herr Russwurm seemed to do a lot of reading in the evening.

'In fact, I think he spends all his time in his study,' he added, with a twinkle in his eye.

'Have you had the chance to talk to him yet?' she asked.

139

'Not yet. But you wait, I might have a question on mining engineering for him one day.'

'I bet you will.' Elisabeth laughed.

In her own home, she was now busy preparing Friedrich and Anja for the new school year. Friedrich was to continue at the school he had attended for a few weeks before the summer break. He was looking forward to it. He was a studious boy who loved learning and Elisabeth was sure that together with his friend Bernd he would enjoy his days there.

For Anja it was going to be a new experience. She was now becoming a proper school girl, starting in Grade one at the 'Volksschule'.

Elisabeth was aware of the tradition in Germany to give school beginners a 'Zuckertüte' on their first day at school. This was a large cardboard cone, elaborately decorated and filled with all sorts of goodies and maybe some writing utensils. It was meant to 'sweeten' the 'serious life' about to start for the children. In Glogau, Elisabeth had often seen these first-graders filing out of school with their Zuckertüte in their arms. She still remembered Friedrich proudly carrying his, and she had been looking forward to this special little event for Anja.

But where could she find a Zuckertüte here? She asked in several shops, but always got the same answer: 'Sorry, we haven't got any this year.'

What should she do? She couldn't disappoint Anja. She was quite determined to get one for her. If she wasn't able to buy one then she would try and make one. When she told Friedrich about it, he had a brilliant idea. He remembered seeing cardboard paper in Herr

Meyerding's printing shop. Surely, he would let them have a little?

'Let's go over together,' Elisabeth suggested, 'and see Gerda and baby Ruth first.'

As luck would have it, Herr Meyerding was visiting his little granddaughter upstairs, while his wife had gone out on errands. They certainly didn't want to run into her again.

When Elisabeth presented her predicament, Herr Meyderding was only too happy to help. He got up and beckoned to Friedrich: 'Come along, we'll have a look and see what we can do.'

Elisabeth noticed Friedrich's excitement, when he glanced back at her.

It wasn't long before the two returned, Friedrich carrying a big cardboard cone that Herr Meyerding had cut out and pasted together.

'Oh, Herr Meyerding!' Elisabeth didn't know what to say.

'Well, it's a great pleasure,' the old man was beaming. 'School beginners must have their Zuckertüte – otherwise they won't go back to school the next day.'

'Look, what Herr Meyerding has given me,' Friedrich showed Elisabeth a handful of coloured pencils. 'I can draw pictures on the cone with these.'

'Yes, of course. That'll be great.'

Elisabeth jumped up and grasped Herr Meyerding's hand: 'Thank you so much.'

He smiled at her: 'Oh, you're welcome. But you'll have to fill the Zuckertüte up, I'm afraid.'

'Yes, we will. I'm sure we'll find something. Anja will love it.'

Back home, Frau Kuhrau – being made an 'accomplice' in this little secret venture – took the cone into her bedroom, and over the next few days Friedrich spent some time there decorating it with colourful pictures. Elisabeth hadn't realized her son's talent. The Zuckertüte looked almost a professional product when he had finished with it.

She was disappointed, though, that she hadn't found more things to fill it up with. There were just a few bonbons, and Opa had brought two special rolls from the bakery and a tiny loaf of bread that he had shaped into a little pretzel. In a stationer's shop Elisabeth had found a second-hand wooden pencil holder with a pencil and a small eraser.

At least the Zuckertüte wasn't too heavy to carry and it looked so lovely with Friedrich's pictures. She couldn't wait to give it to her little daughter on her first day at school.

26

The Second Postcard

Elisabeth was glad to see her children happily settled at school. She noticed Friedrich's eagerness to absorb knowledge. He was keen to share it not only with her but also with the other householders at Brechtstrasse 8.

One afternoon he came rushing upstairs excitedly, with a heavy book under his arm.

'Look, what Frau Kuhrau has given me,' he called out to his mother.

'What is it?'

'It's a famous story, called "Lederstrumpf". Do you know it?'

'No, I don't. Let me see. What is it about?'

Friedrich put the book on the table: 'It's about an American Indian boy with the nickname "leather stockings". Frau Kuhrau said I would like it.'

Elisabeth smiled. Frau Kuhrau certainly knew what an enthusiastic boy like Friedrich would enjoy. She must have observed his perceptiveness and interest.

'How lovely.' Elisabeth took the book in her hand. 'It's a big book. That's going to keep you occupied for a long time.'

'Yes. And I can borrow more books when I've finished with this one.'

'That's wonderful. You like reading, don't you, Friedrich?'

Elisabeth felt very touched. There seemed to be no end to this family's kindness.

Anja had made a good start at school, too. Elisabeth was surprised that she had found a little boyfriend almost immediately. It emerged that Andreas had obviously been fascinated with Anja's Zuckertüte and had made a beeline for her in the playground on their first day. He lived only a short distance away from them. Elisabeth met his mother, and they agreed to let the children walk to and from school together. Andreas called for Anja every morning, and it was lovely for Elisabeth to see the two companions toddle off. Anja was the taller of the two. Would she outgrow her mother one day? Elisabeth had often wished she'd been a bit taller, especially after marrying her six foot plus husband.

But where was this tall husband of hers? The days were flying by. It was now late September. He hadn't written again. Had he tried to cross the border and been arrested? She didn't dare think of it.

It appeared that people were crossing the border in both directions all the time. Elisabeth had read reports in the paper about attempted escapes. A man, aged 74, had tried three times to get across, and each time had been caught, ending up in a cellar without food. He was made to work for the Russian guards, cutting wood, before being sent back. Had he tried again and succeeded? Of course, no one here in the East would ever know. How much longer would she have to wait for Ludwig?

One late morning, while she was putting her shopping away, she was suddenly alerted to a droning sound from outside. She listened: within a slow regular rhythm she could recognize a simple tune. A funeral march? As she stepped towards the window to have a look, she heard Lotte call her name:

'Come down quickly, Elisabeth, something is going on outside.'

She rushed downstairs and was dumbfounded by what she encountered. A long procession of Russian soldiers in their military uniforms was slowly marching past their house, following a gun carriage, which bore an open coffin.

Elisabeth shrank back and turned to Lotte: 'Who might that be?'

Lotte shrugged her shoulder: 'A high ranking personality, I gather.'

'It's a general, according to his uniform,' a bystander explained. 'Can you see his big cap lying at his feet? They'll place that inside the coffin at the burial.'

Elisabeth turned to the man beside her: 'Have you seen something like this before?'

'Yes, indeed, I have. In Russia itself. The Russians make a lot of their funerals.'

Elisabeth was taken aback by the man's words. She looked at him closely. 'When were you in Russia?'

'I was a prisoner of war there, but I had the good fortune to be released on medical grounds.'

Glancing around, Elisabeth noticed a lot of people lining the street, whispering to each other. Surely, no one had ever seen such a spectacle here before.

She turned to Lotte: 'I wonder where they are going to take him?'

'Oh, probably to the big cemetery. I bet the Russians have reserved a special section for themselves there.

They seem to be taking over the whole town now.'

'Yes,' Elisabeth agreed. 'Have you seen their luxurious form of transport? When I passed the building of the Secret Police the other day, I saw that the wrought-iron gate was boarded up from the inside. Just as I was crossing the road, the gate slowly opened and an enormous limousine emerged. It moved so fast and smooth. I could just see three men in grey suits, staring straight ahead.'

The funeral procession had by now moved past them, and the music was slowly fading away.

'Oh, Elisabeth, what have we come to? At least, in the war, we were all Germans here. But now? How long will these Russians stay and rule over us?'

Elisabeth was stunned to hear such a despondent tone in Lotte's voice. She had always admired her optimism and her ability to see the bright side of things. The difficult circumstances in her home town seemed to have taken their toll even on her now.

They were just turning to go back into the house, when Elisabeth spotted Gerda running towards them. She was waving frantically, holding something in her hand that looked like a letter. Elisabeth's heart stood still. Could it be another message from Ludwig?

'Here you are,' Gerda tried to get her breath back as she handed Elisabeth the letter. It was indeed from Ludwig. Elisabeth ripped the envelope open and took out a postcard. The three of them stepped inside the front door, as she read it out:

Just to let you know we are fine here. Am very busy. Have visited Frau Beuermann, had tea with her. Played chess on Monday (3:1). Hope Friedrich and Anja are good and doing their homework. Weather fine here. Days are getting shorter. Keep counting the sheep. Father sends his love with mine. L.'

'He's talking about the *Counting of the Sheep* again,' Gerda observed.

'Yes, he is. He's certainly determined to make it over here.' Elisabeth looked at her friends: 'I really don't know what will happen.' But at least he is safe, she thought, or was when he wrote this.

As soon as she was on her own upstairs, she read the letter again. She wondered who *Frau Beuermann* was. Perhaps someone who would help him get across the border? And what about: *'Days are getting shorter'*? Did this have a double meaning?

She wasn't surprised that Ludwig had already found a chess club in Eschwege. Of course he'd won the game. He always did. Her husband, the Silesian Chess Master, would only play to win.

She sat down, letting her eyes wander around the room. It looked so pleasant. It had become a real 'home' very quickly for the three of them. Would they have to leave soon? How would the children react? She wasn't going to tell them anything yet. It would only unsettle them.

While she was still musing about what her future would bring, she heard footsteps on the stairs. That was Anja, home from school. She quickly put the letter away, opened the door and with a joyful 'hello, darling', she took her little daughter in her arms.

27

Ludwig – Here at Last

Ludwig's second letter gave Elisabeth great hope that her family would be reunited at last. Reading it over and over again, she became convinced that Ludwig would try everything in his power to come and take his family to Eschwege in West Germany, where he was now living with his father and where they could start a new life together in freedom.

In retrospect, she could now see what a blessing it was that Ludwig's father had been so adamant to stay behind when they left Glogau. She remembered Ludwig telling her on his brief visit last Spring that his father had eventually been persuaded by a friend to join her on one of the last trains out of their home town, before the rail tracks were blown up. This friend had then taken him to the little town in the county of Hesse, just beyond the border that now divided Germany.

Here, in Russian occupied East Germany, circumstances were not improving. On the contrary, Elisabeth felt that life seemed to become more difficult by the day. An increased sense of being closed in and watched over by the Russian Secret Police was spreading among the population. Houses were still being searched for former German soldiers, often in the middle of the night.

Food continued to be drastically rationed and Elisabeth found it hard to feed her growing children properly. How lucky that her father was still working in the bakery, which meant he frequently brought her an extra loaf of bread or some flour.

As the days were getting shorter – it was now the beginning of October – she often went to see her parents after the children had gone to bed.

One Monday evening she found her brother Fredo there. She was pleased to see him and exchange some news with him. As he lived quite a distance away from her in the town they didn't see very much of each other. There were so many questions to ask: *How was his daughter Gisela getting on?* She had started school at the same time as Anja. *Had he begun with his teachers' training course yet? And how about Liesel, his wife? Had she found work as a dressmaker?*

Before long the conversation turned to Ludwig's recent letter. Elisabeth couldn't conceal her excitement about it.

Fredo said: 'You sound very sure that he'll get across the border soon.'

She looked at her brother slightly taken aback. Had she heard a hint of doubt in his voice?

'Well, yes, I'm hoping he'll be here soon ,' she replied.

Fredo hesitated before going on: 'I don't want to dash your hopes, but I've only just heard that the guarding of the border has been tightened severely in the last few days. It appears that thousands of people are now trying to cross over and many have been arrested and then sent back.'

Elisabeth shuddered. Please, no! In a trembling voice she said: 'Oh, Fredo, you're frightening me. I know

Ludwig is trying to get here. I can't bear the thought that something might happen to him.'

'Well, let's not give up hope,' Elisabeth's mother had been listening to them anxiously. 'There must be people who do get through. Why shouldn't Ludwig manage it?'

'You're right,' Elisabeth was glad to hear her mother speaking so positively. 'I'm sure he'll make it.'

She now saw her mother putting a plate with a few small slices of poppy seed cake on the table. She knew whose favourite cake that was.

'Where on earth did you get this?' Fredo gazed at the plate, astonished.

'Well, they seem to work little miracles at the bakery,' his mother laughed looking at her husband.

'You won't believe this,' Opa said with a big grin on his face, 'the other day I happened to look into an old cupboard in the bake house and found several tins that hadn't been opened for a long time, it seemed. I showed them to Frau Mettler, the baker's wife. She was very surprised and said her husband must have put them there ages ago, before he was called up. They were tightly closed, and on opening them, we found the poppy seeds which were perfectly all right. So we made a few cakes.'

'Brilliant!' Fredo exclaimed.

Elisabeth smiled, remembering how in their younger days her brother could never wait to get his teeth into his beloved poppy seed cake.

'I made two extra cakes, so you can both take one home for your families,' Opa said.

'Oh, Father, what would we do without you?' Elisabeth was as pleased as her brother, 'the children will love it.'

When they left their parents, Fredo accompanied Elisabeth across the green to her house. Saying 'goodbye', he hugged her gently: 'I do hope that Ludwig will be here soon in spite of what I told you earlier.'

'Thank you, Fredo, and I hope I have good news for you before long. Give my love to your family. All the very best to you.'

Elisabeth went up and opened the door to her room carefully, anxious not to wake the children. She heard them breathing regularly. They were sleeping soundly after their usual active day.

But sleep would not come to her. Her head was spinning with imagined pictures of Ludwig's journey across the border. Was he perhaps sitting in a cellar, watched over by a Russian guard threatening him with a rifle? Was he running across a field, trying to escape the shooting? Or was he hiding in a wood, waiting until all noises had died down before he dared make a dash for the border?

What did the border look like? Was it just a path with barriers? Did it run alongside an old railway track? A picture she had seen in a paper some time ago now started to haunt her. It showed a man ducking under a small bridge staring behind him with wide eyes, as if he expected to be caught at any moment.

She tossed and turned, getting hot under her sheets.

A coughing noise from Anja's bed made her jump. Surely, Anja couldn't have caught a cold? It was still very warm during these early October days and Elisabeth was pleased that the children had been able to play outside in the afternoons. She listened intently for a while. Everything was quiet now.

She lay back, trying hard to calm herself down. It must be well after midnight, and she needed some sleep. Tomorrow morning she was going to visit an Old People's Home. She had been told there might be a job going. She wasn't too keen on it, but she would take the post if they accepted her. She needed the money.

Suddenly she heard a loud bang. Was it shooting? Had someone called her name? She was shaking. She opened her eyes. It was still dark. Had she been dreaming? She sat up in her bed, shivering all over.

There was a soft knock on the door and then a familiar voice: Elisabeth?

She jumped out of bed, tore the door open and with a suppressed scream fell into Ludwig's arms.

Fortunately, the children had slept through the night's event. When they started stirring in the morning, Elisabeth quickly went over to their beds.

'Hush,' she whispered, 'be very quiet.'

'What's the matter?' Friedrich demanded to know.

'Something wonderful has happened in the night. Look, who's over there.'

Both children peered with wide eyes, stretching their necks, and in an instant Anja was out of her bed, shouting: 'Daddy!'

Elisabeth was unable to stop her dashing across the room, with Friedrich following.

Ludwig woke with a start and sat up, leaning over to take both his children in his arms: 'Here you are. I've found you at last.'

In their excitement, the children jumped onto his bed, almost suffocating their father with hugs and kisses.

'Careful, careful, you'll break the bed.' Elisabeth had trouble making herself heard.

But for once they didn't listen. They were overjoyed to have their father back. They showered him with questions: *When had he come into the room? Had he had a long journey? How had he found his way here in the dark? Was he going to stay with them now?*

Elisabeth could see how overwhelmed Ludwig was with his children clinging to him. He looked so tired. She noticed that he had lost a lot of weight. She quickly got dressed and started making breakfast. Then she called out firmly: 'You must let your father rest now. He is very tired and needs more sleep. Get yourselves ready and have something to eat.'

'Do we have to go to school today?' Anja asked in a whining tone.

'Of course you do,' a strong male voice rang out, 'I want to know what you've learnt when you come back.'

Elisabeth was glad to have her husband's authority to support her. Anja didn't say another word and obediently let her mother send her on her way.

By the time the children had gone to school Ludwig was fast asleep. So Elisabeth left the room quietly and went down to talk to Frau Kuhrau and Lotte, who were having breakfast in the kitchen.

'Oh, Elisabeth, have you recovered from your shock?' Lotte pointed to a chair for her to join them.

'Yes, I think so, but I still can't believe Ludwig is here. You must have been terribly frightened. I didn't hear the bell. What happened?'

'Well,' Lotte began, 'I was getting myself a drink in the kitchen. It was nearly two o'clock. Just as I was

153

going upstairs, the bell went. I froze. For a moment I just stood there, listening. After a while there was a knock. I peered through the little window by the front door. The moonlight was quite bright and when I saw a tall man with a rucksack I knew it couldn't be the Secret Police. I called out "Who are you?" and – well, you know who he was.'

'Yes,' Elisabeth couldn't help smiling. 'Actually, Ludwig went to the Meyerdings first. He told me he climbed over that high wooden gate at the side of their house and then rang the bell. He waited a long time before the old Herr Meyerding opened the door and told him where we were.'

Frau Kuhrau had been listening intently: 'I bet the old man had a great shock, as well?'

'I'm sure he had.' Elisabeth agreed, 'but I think he quickly recognized Ludwig, as he had met him earlier in the year.'

'I wonder how your husband found his way in the dark from the station?' Frau Kuhrau asked, 'it's a fair distance from here.'

'Yes, but don't forget Ludwig was here in the spring,' Elisabeth explained. 'He will have remembered quite a bit. He has a good sense of direction. He told me he had to be ever so careful when he first got off the train. There were uniformed men patrolling the platforms. He thought they were Russians. He was desperate not to be spotted, so he quickly locked himself into the men's lavatory and stayed there for almost an hour. Eventually it all went quiet and he started on his way here.'

'Elisabeth, what a feat! You should be very proud of your husband.'

'You're right. And I am!' Elisabeth nodded. 'I've yet to hear, though, how exactly he got across the border. It's taken him several days.'

'Really? Oh, I hope it won't be such a long journey when you go back with the children,' Lotte sounded very concerned.

Frau Kuhrau looked at Elisabeth with sad eyes: 'It will be so quiet without you all.'

'And Bernd and Ingrid will be devastated to lose their playmates,' Lotte added, 'they've been getting on so well together, haven't they?'

'I know. Now that we've found such a good home here with you we've got to leave. It doesn't seem right, somehow.' Elisabeth felt close to tears. Would she ever find friends like Lotte and Frau Kuhrau who had shown her so much kindness and support over many months?

'But we'll stay in touch, that's a promise,' she said. 'In any case, I hope we'll be able to come back and visit my parents before too long. They seem to have settled in well with the Russwurms. I don't think I need to worry about them at the moment.'

'We'll make sure they're all right.' Lotte smiled at Elisabeth.

'Thank you, Lotte. It is so good to know you'll be near them.'

'I suppose you'll have to start packing up now?' Frau Kuhrau asked.

'Yes, as soon as Ludwig gets up we'll discuss everything. He said we'll be leaving on Thursday, the day after tomorrow.'

'Let us know how we can help. Do you need another case, perhaps?'

'Oh, that's very kind of you, but I think we'll manage. Ludwig has brought an extra holdall. And those little rucksacks we made in Glogau will come into their own again. Do you remember, Lotte?'

'Yes, I do,' Lotte smiled, 'that's almost a year ago now. Hasn't time flown?'

When Elisabeth went up to their room she found Ludwig sitting at the table helping himself to bread and jam and some coffee she had left in a flask for him. She walked over and put her arms around him: 'Oh, darling, is it really true you're here?'

'Yes, sweetheart, it is,' he looked up at her lovingly, 'I can hardly believe it myself. It's taken such a long time.'

Elisabeth sat down with him and asked: 'When did you leave Eschwege?'

'Last Wednesday. I tell you, it was quite an odyssey. I thought I'd be able to cross over at a place near Bad Harzburg. But that proved impossible. The border was so heavily guarded on both sides. I tried several times, with a number of other people. But each time we were driven back.

Elisabeth looked at her husband, horrified: 'Oh, Ludwig, what did you do then?'

'I had heard people mention a place called Hötensleben where it might be easier to get across. But that meant I had to go back to Bad Harzburg, and from there on to Braunschweig and then to Helmstedt.'

Elisabeth shook her head in disbelief: 'What a long tour! Where did you sleep?'

'Well, mostly in station waiting rooms. In Helmstedt I found a little hotel next to the station. So I stayed there on Sunday.'

'And how did you actually get across the border?' Elisabeth was getting impatient.

'Well, yesterday morning, Monday, I boarded a train for Schöningen. From there it meant walking. It turned out to be a long march. Again I found myself in a little crowd of people some of whom seemed to know the way very well. So I tacked on to them. No one spoke much. First we walked along the railway line, and then a long way through a wood. I couldn't see any guards. Eventually, after about an hour and a half, we reached a little stream. We waded through, and that was it. A man said – almost jokingly – "Welcome to East Germany".'

'You had to wade through a stream?' Elisabeth stared at Ludwig.

'Yes, but it was only about ten metres wide and not very deep. Then we walked on, and suddenly someone grabbed me by my arm and pushed me into dense undergrowth, indicating to me not to speak. He had obviously spotted a Russian guard. We held our breath. After about twenty minutes the same man beckoned to me and we continued walking. I dare say I would never have made it without these people.'

Elisabeth could hardly believe what she was hearing.

'And did you find that place Hötensleben all right?' she asked.

'Yes, that was easy. I caught a train from there almost immediately. I changed twice and got into Quedlinburg just after midnight. So – here I am.'

Elisabeth was quite dazed: 'Oh Ludwig. What a journey! And we've got to do the same in reverse on Thursday?'

'Yes, darling, but don't be frightened. We'll make it, I promise!' He went over to her, took her in his arms and kissed her tenderly.

Suddenly Elisabeth felt warm and secure and confident. 'Yes, we'll make it,' she said quietly.

28

Preparing to Leave Quedlinburg

Elisabeth was busy sorting out clothes for packing, when the children arrived back from school. Anja was home first. Elisabeth could hear her rushing up the stairs. She burst in, looked around the room and cried out:

'Where is Daddy?'

'He'll be here in a minute,' Elisabeth tried to calm her down, ' he's gone over to the Meyerdings to invite Ruth and her mummy round this afternoon.'

'Why?' Anja looked at her, baffled.

Elisabeth knew that she couldn't leave it any longer to tell her little girl what was going to happen.

'We have to say goodbye to them.'

'Are they going away?' Anja sounded even more puzzled.

Elisabeth put a pile of clothes on one side and turned to her: 'No, they are not going away, but we are.'

'Oh Mummy, where are we going?' Anja rushed up to her throwing her arms around her.

'You see, Daddy has come to take us to West Germany where Opa Giertz lives. And we're going to live with him there now.'

Anja looked at her with wide eyes. Elisabeth realized how confusing all this must be for her. Could she see tears welling up in her eyes?

Anja asked: 'Why doesn't Opa Giertz come and live with us here? I don't want to go away.'

Elisabeth made her sit down and put an arm around her: 'I know, sweetheart. One day you'll understand and you'll be very happy. You see, our country is now divided, and it will be so much better for us to live in West Germany under the Americans. They are good to the people and don't go round arresting them as the Russians do here.'

Anja had a very earnest look on her face now. She seemed to be remembering something: 'A boy at school told us his uncle was taken from his house in the night.'

Elisabeth was quite shocked to hear her say this. She replied: 'Well, I can only think it was because the man was a German soldier. And you know that Daddy was a soldier, don't you?'

'Will they take Daddy away?' Anja looked up at her with fear in her eyes.

'No, they won't,' Elisabeth tried to be as reassuring as possible. 'They don't even know he is here. But it's important that we go away quickly.'

'When are we going?' Anja still sounded agitated.

'On Thursday morning. So you've only got one more day at school. And you must not tell anybody about this.'

Anja shook her head vehemently: 'No, I won't. I don't want them to take Daddy away.'

'Of course not. We're only telling our friends.'

'Are Oma and Opa coming with us?'

'No, but they'll come later, when we're more settled.'

'Has Opa Giertz got a nice room for us?' Anja asked and Elisabeth thought she heard a hint of excitement in her voice now.

'I don't know, darling, but I'm sure he'll help us find a place.'

Anja got up and started looking at all the things her mother had laid out, ready to be packed. She suddenly spotted her own dirndl dress and picked it up. She held it against herself, laughing: 'It's much too small, Mummy, I can't wear it anymore.'

'No, you can't, dear.' Elisabeth was glad the conversation had taken a lighter turn.

'Do you know what? Shall we leave it here for Ruth? She can wear it when she grows older. Would that be a good idea?'

'Yes,' Anja seemed happy about her mother's suggestion. 'Then she can always think of me.'

She looked at the dress again becoming quite thoughtful: 'But she won't know me, she's only a baby now. Can we come back here and visit her next year?'

'I don't see why not.'

Elisabeth was relieved that Anja had taken the prospect of this drastic change in her life relatively well. At six and a half she showed remarkable understanding. Probably it was due to Friedrich's influence who was mature far beyond his twelve years. Elisabeth knew how much Anja looked up to her brother, and perhaps the two of them had more talks together than she was aware of.

While continuing with the sorting and packing of things, Elisabeth's mind seemed to be a whirlwind. She hadn't anticipated that their time in Quedlinburg would come to such an abrupt end. She was reminded of her hurried departure from Glogau, back in January. This time, though, it was different: she had her man by her side to support her. And she knew she was going to a safe place where they would be able to live together in freedom.

It wouldn't be easy to build up a new life out of nothing. She looked at their few belongings lying in front of her. The children's clothes were so worn and soon they would be far too small. Would she have enough money to buy new ones for them in Eschwege? Would Ludwig get a good job soon? What kind of accommodation were they going to have there?

But she didn't allow herself to linger on these thoughts. She was deeply grateful that they were reunited as a family again. Could she wish for more, when so many other men had not returned to their loved ones after this terrible war? Together they would face and conquer whatever lay ahead.

There were now practically only hours left before their departure, and in a way Elisabeth was glad that their goodbyes had to be kept short. It was very sad to leave so many dear friends behind, but her mind had to be set on the future.

In the afternoon, Gerda called in briefly with Ruth. Anja was very excited. She grabbed her dirndl dress and held it up in front of the gurgling baby, saying: 'Look, I have a present for you.'

Elisabeth could see how touched and delighted Gerda was. She nodded at Elisabeth, and said to Anja: 'Thank you so much. That's lovely. I'll tell Ruth who gave that to her when she's old enough to understand.'

Elisabeth looked at mother and baby, remembering the day in May when she had accompanied Gerda to the maternity clinic where Ruth was born. When would she see them again?

Later they all went to Oma and Opa and Elisabeth was reminded in a flash of her mother's encouraging words, spoken barely twenty-four hours ago: "Why shouldn't Ludwig manage to get across the border?" Here he stood, having indeed managed it.

Hearing about their imminent departure, her parents immediately offered to help. Oma was going to make them sandwiches for their journey and Opa would accompany the family to the station.

In the morning of their last day at school Elisabeth warned both her children that on no account were they to tell anybody that they would not return the following day. Nodding, they both whispered at the door: 'No, we won't,' looking back at her almost mischievously. Ludwig had not told them any details about his dramatic border crossing, in order not to frighten them and it seemed to Elisabeth that both were getting quite excited. Maybe it was best to let them think of their forthcoming journey as an adventure rather than a potentially dangerous escape.

While the children were at school, Elisabeth took Ludwig to see her brother and his family. Walking in, Elisabeth beamed at Fredo, remembering their parting words two nights before. He took his sister in his arms, saying: 'Elisabeth, how wonderful. I'm so happy for you. I'll miss you, but I hope we'll be able to join you in the not too distant future.'

'Yes, Fredo,' Elisabeth replied, 'It'll be marvellous to see you all in the West before long.'

Fredo was interested to hear some details of Ludwig's military service, and it was only now that Elisabeth learned that Ludwig's Air Force Unit had been transferred to Schleswig-Holstein at the end of the war.

That region was occupied by the British, and thus he had found himself in British captivity. When it came to his release at the beginning of August, Ludwig had asked to be sent to Eschwege, in West Germany, where his father was living. This was granted, and he boarded a freight train provided for the freed prisoners of war.

Elisabeth looked at him in amazement as she listened.

But Ludwig laughed: 'Yes, it was actually a transport train for cattle. But we didn't mind at all. We were free. Nothing else mattered. And of course I was hoping to bring my family over as soon as possible.'

Elisabeth gave a relieved smile. Her thoughts went back to that day in January when she had tried to persuade her father-in-law to join her. What if he hadn't stood so firm then? He would probably be with them here now. Instead, he was waiting for their arrival in free West Germany.

On their way back, Elisabeth and Ludwig called on a few friends to say goodbye, and then it was time to do the last bit of packing.

Anja came home from school, excited about a pencil her teacher had given her: 'He said I can do my homework with it but I must bring it back tomorrow.'

Elisabeth turned to her in great alarm: 'What did you say?'

'I only said "Yes, thank you, Herr Krause". He smiled and said "Till tomorrow." But I won't go back, will I?'

'No, you won't'. Elisabeth heaved a sigh of relief. Obviously Anja hadn't given anything away. 'We'd better leave that pencil here for Ingrid.'

The last night in Quedlinburg had arrived. Elisabeth fell into bed, dead tired. Their cases and rucksacks stood ready by the door. They were to catch an early train. Tomorrow they would start their journey to freedom.

29

Approaching the Border

Elisabeth woke with a start.

'It's time to get up,' she heard Ludwig say. For a moment she didn't know where she was. Had she slept that deeply? There were Friedrich and Anja standing by her bedside, ready dressed.

'Mummy, get up quickly,' Anja bent over giving her a big kiss. 'We'll miss the train.'

In an instant Elisabeth was out of bed. 'You're right, darling. I'll be ever so quick.' She flew about, getting herself ready and putting the last few things into her big handbag.

While Ludwig and the children carried their luggage down, Elisabeth looked around the room for a last time. She had felt very much at home here. Where would she be tonight?

She quickly followed the others into the kitchen where Lotte and Frau Kuhrau had laid out a little breakfast. There was bread and jam and even a slice of cheese for each of them. Elisabeth saw how pleased Ludwig was to have a big cup of coffee. He'd always loved his coffee and today it would give him extra energy.

It wasn't long before the doorbell went. There were Opa and Oma. It was time to say goodbye. Elisabeth couldn't help thinking of that morning in February when she had left her parents in the care of kind Frau

Lehmann in Spremberg and she was grateful that here, too, were friends on whose help they could call, when she was far away.

After warm hugs and many farewell wishes, the four of them were on their way to the station, accompanied by Opa. Walking across the big square Kleers, Elisabeth kept looking back to the house, remembering the day she and the children had arrived there, tired and anxious about what would happen to them.

When they got near to the station, Friedrich suddenly said: 'There's pastor Zaremba on the other side of the road.' He waved to him, and the pastor, who recognized Friedrich, waved back with a smile. Elisabeth and Ludwig also smiled at him, and Elisabeth noticed that he was looking at their luggage with interest. Was he guessing where this family was travelling?

Elisabeth wondered if they would have difficulty buying their tickets. She needn't have worried. Ludwig got exactly what he asked for, and soon they were standing on the platform.

'Now here is some food for the journey to keep you going,' Opa said with a smile, handing a big packet to Elisabeth.

'Thank you, Father, this is wonderful.'

'I hope you enjoy the poppy seed cake, too. I made it for you yesterday.'

Elisabeth could see Anja's eyes lighting up when she heard Opa's words. Like her uncle Fredo she was particularly fond of poppy seed cake.

'Thank you, Opa,' she rushed into his arms, and he held her close to him, kissing her gently. Elisabeth knew how much he would miss her. It was good to know his other little granddaughter, Gisela, was still staying on in Quedlinburg.

With a loud puffing noise the train pulled in. This time boarding was easy for Elisabeth and the children. They had two strong men to lift the luggage in, and in contrast to their previous travels they weren't pushed by huge crowds of people. They had a compartment almost to themselves. As the train started moving, they all pressed against the window, waving goodbye to Opa. He waved back and Elisabeth could see tears running down his cheeks. When would they meet again?

By mid-morning they reached Halberstadt, where they had to change trains. Elisabeth reminded Ludwig of the bombing of this town in April, during his brief visit in Quedlinburg: 'Can you remember the strange smell of burning when we were walking in the afternoon?'

'Yes,' he replied, 'and all those little pieces of paper fluttering down.'

Now it was October and, from what Elisabeth could see, the town still lay in ruins. She was horrified. How many German towns would look like this? And Glogau, her home town? Of course, that didn't belong to Germany anymore.

Their next stop was Oschersleben, where they would have to change trains again. Elisabeth was full of admiration for her husband. He seemed so confident and knew exactly where to go and from which platform the next train would leave.

'Are we nearly there, Daddy?' Anja was getting impatient with being rushed along platforms and having to get in and out of trains.

'Yes, my darling,' Elisabeth heard Ludwig's calm and reassuring voice, 'it won't be long now. We're coming into Hornhausen. From there it's only half an hour to Hötensleben. That's where we get out. Then we just have to walk for a little while.'

He smiled at her, but Elisabeth could see how confusing all these explanations were for Anja.

'Let's have something to eat,' she suggested, reaching for Opa's food packet.

'Oh yes, please,' Ludwig and the children shouted with one voice.

While munching away on Oma's sandwiches and Opa's poppy seed cake and watching beautiful autumn-coloured woods fly by, they looked contented. But Elisabeth gradually felt a considerable nervousness creeping up on her. By now they were in their fourth train since leaving Quedlinburg. They couldn't be that far from the border anymore? She kept her anxiety to herself. She mustn't alarm the children. Ludwig had told Anja they would have to walk for a while. Looking at their luggage, she hoped it wasn't going to be for long.

She checked the time on her watch. It was almost half past three. At that moment the train started slowing down and then pulled into a little station. A big sign read: Hötensleben. This was the place. The name had engrained itself in her mind ever since Ludwig had described his dramatic border crossing to her.

Elisabeth could hear the loudspeaker: 'Hötensleben – Everyone please get off. The train ends here.' Carrying a case in one hand and holding Anja's hand tightly with the other, she followed Ludwig and Friedrich to the exit. They certainly weren't alone. There were dozens of people like them, carrying their belongings in cases, cardboard boxes and rucksacks.

Outside the station building they were approached by strangers who seemed to know why they had come here. A friendly looking young man came up to Ludwig and Elisabeth and asked: 'Would you like to come with me? I'm sure I'll be able to help you.'

Elisabeth looked at Ludwig, stunned. Ludwig answered the man: 'Well, we'll be grateful, if you think you can help us?'

'Yes, definitely,' the man nodded, 'we live here, and we know the movements of the border guards. You'll be quite all right. We'll help you get across.'

Elisabeth and Ludwig exchanged looks, still taken aback. Then they all followed the man to his house, a few hundred yards away. His wife was waiting and said it wouldn't be long before the changing of the guards. She was sure the next one was one who could be bribed to let them cross over.

'And what should we give him?' Elisabeth asked anxiously.

'Well, they all like alcohol, of course, and perhaps a piece of jewellery. I see, you have a gold wristwatch.'

Elisabeth was glad she was wearing it and agreed only too willingly to sacrifice it.

The man said to Ludwig: 'I can sell you a bottle of Schnapps.'

'Yes, please,' Ludwig answered, 'as long as it helps us to get across.'

Elisabeth thought that ten marks was rather a lot of money. She wondered how much these people were making for themselves.

Hötensleben

Soon they were on their way. The young man led them to a large park. In the distance Elisabeth could see a grand manor house. Had the Russians occupied that for themselves? Beautiful old trees lined the wide path. After a while they turned into a narrow footpath. At a junction the man stopped and said he couldn't go any further. He pointed into the direction they had to follow: 'Continue straight on. Can you see those two oak trees? From there it's only 100 metres to a little stream. That's the border. Wade through and you'll be there. Good luck.'

With that he turned round, and Elisabeth saw him waving back to them. They were on their own. Slowly and carefully they walked on, Ludwig leading the way. Elisabeth thought of the stream. Ludwig had told her about that. Would they make it? They didn't speak. Elisabeth could see how frightened Anja looked. She felt how her little girl was clinging to her. Elisabeth smiled at her reassuringly.

Suddenly a most terrible scream rang through the trees: 'Zu—rück! Zu—rück' (Back! Back!).Elisabeth saw a Russian guard running towards them, waving his machine gun over his head.

They stopped, turned round and ran as fast as they could, for about fifty metres. Ludwig shouted: 'In here, quick.' They dived into some dense bushes. The guard screamed again: 'Zu—rück!', but Elisabeth noticed he had not followed them. They huddled together, holding on to each other and to their cases. They listened. Everything was quiet now.

Ludwig said: 'It's no use. We have to go back. That wasn't the right guard.'

So they got up and quickly walked back to the village.

30

Crossing the Border

When they knocked on the door of the house they had left just under an hour ago, their kind helpers didn't seem overly surprised.

'I'm sorry,' the man said, 'there must have been a sudden change-around of guards. You'll make it later. Come in and wait here.'

No sooner had they sat down at a big farmer's-kitchen table than Elisabeth heard another knock on the door. A neighbour was calling, talking of his own 'travellers' bad luck. Elisabeth sensed that a real trafficking business was going on here. Were these villagers supplementing their income in this way? She thought again of the high price Ludwig had paid the man for the bottle of Schnapps.

She could see how weary the children looked. What an experience for them! How long would they have to wait here?

As if the man's wife had guessed her thoughts, she came in and put a jug of apple juice and a plate of biscuits on the table, saying: 'Help yourselves.'

'How very kind of you, thank you,' Elisabeth looked up at her. 'I only hope we don't have to disturb you much longer.'

'That's all right,' the woman seemed quite relaxed. 'Have a little rest. The guards will change soon, and then you can go.'

'Are there many people wanting to cross over?' Elisabeth was intrigued to know more about this strange border life.

'Oh yes, a great lot, every day. They all want to go to the West. There won't be many people left here soon. Where are you going?'

Elisabeth let Ludwig take over the conversation: 'We're going to my father in Eschwege. He is on his own, you see.'

'Oh, I've been to Eschwege many times, before they put the border up,' the woman became quite interested. 'I expect your father has a house there?'

'No, he hasn't,' Ludwig answered, and Elisabeth could hear sadness in his voice: 'We're all refugees from Silesia. We've lost everything. These cases and rucksacks are all we have.'

Elisabeth saw dismay on the woman's face as she asked: 'So you haven't even got a place to go to?'

'I'm afraid not, but I'm sure my father will help us find something soon.'

'I hope so, and…' Her words were cut short by her husband, who came rushing in, calling out: 'The coast is clear now. The guards have changed. This one will let you through. Come, I'll lead you out again.'

They all jumped up, grabbed their bags, shouted goodbye to the woman and followed the man on to the now almost familiar route. Elisabeth held Anja's hand again as they hurried along the path through the park. There was the manor house, and there were the two oak trees. Soon the man stopped, pointed in the direction of the stream and turned back, waving to them.

They walked on, looking straight ahead. It was

exactly as the man had told them earlier: another hundred metres through trees, and there was the stream. But how would they get across? Elisabeth thought it looked quite deep. It was about ten metres wide.

Suddenly a clicking noise made them stop in their tracks. They stared at each other.

Then Elisabeth spotted him: a tall Russian guard, in a long, greenish coat and a big cap with a red star on the front, a rifle strapped over his shoulder. He stood about twenty metres to their right. Elisabeth stared at him, frozen. He beckoned to them, silently, pointing to a spot in the stream where they should cross.

They ran towards him. Elisabeth quickly slipped off her watch and handed it over. The guard took it, smiling broadly at her. She now pointed to Ludwig, who gave him the bottle of Schnapps. With a big grin the guard put it in the pocket of his coat.

The next moment Ludwig had stepped into the water, which came up to his knees. He was carrying the biggest case. Elisabeth followed and tried to help hold the case up. Friedrich was also in the water, carrying the smaller case. He was the quickest and reached the opposite side first.

In the confusion Elisabeth had let go of Anja's hand. She thought her daughter was right behind her, but when she looked back she saw her standing next to the guard. Horrified, she shouted: 'Ludwig, quick, get Anja over here!'

She had never seen him react so fast. A few steps through the splashing water, and he was back on the other side. Elisabeth watched as the guard lifted Anja on Ludwig's shoulders, piggyback. Her heart stood still.

What if the guard had kept Anja with him? She could see how frightened Anja looked. Her woollen cap had slipped off her head and was hanging loosely round her neck. It took Elisabeth a few seconds before she got her breath back. The guard waved to them and walked away.

On this side of the stream the embankment was steeper and very slippery, and they struggled hard to get out of the water. Suddenly Elisabeth heard voices. Someone said in English: 'Come on, we'll help you.'

She looked up and saw two British soldiers smiling at them. They pulled them up and helped carry their bags, which were now soaking wet. The soldiers pushed them across the path and towards what looked like an arboretum. One said: 'Quick, hide in there! Our border patrol will be here any minute.' With that they disappeared.

Elisabeth and the family ran and tried to hide. But to no avail. They had been spotted. A jeep came to a screeching halt and two British officers jumped out. One of them commanded (in perfect German): 'Please, come out of there, straight away!'

Elisabeth's heart sank. There was no getting away. They had escaped the Russians. Were they now to be captured by the British? She looked at Ludwig, terrified. But he said calmly: 'It'll be all right.'

In no time they found themselves squeezed into the jeep that took them to the nearby British border checkpoint. There Elisabeth saw about thirty other German people who had obviously also been picked up by the patrols. What a bedraggled lot!

They were ordered to line up in front of the officers, one of whom started interrogating them individually.

An old woman who was standing near to Elisabeth was wailing: 'You can shoot me dead on the spot, I'm not going back to Ivan.' Elisabeth saw the officer looking at her in consternation, and then heard him talking quietly to her.

Soon it was their turn to be questioned, and Elisabeth couldn't have been more grateful to have her husband by her side. When the officer asked rather abruptly: 'Why have you come here?' she was surprised to hear Ludwig's calm and measured tone of voice as he answered: 'I have been living in West Germany since my release from British captivity.'

He showed the officer his residence permit which he had carried in an inside pocket of his coat. Pointing to Elisabeth and the children he continued: 'I hope you have sympathy for my situation, as I want to be reunited with my wife and two children.'

Elisabeth watched anxiously as the officer examined Ludwig's papers with a serious look on his face. He seemed to be thinking hard before he replied in a grave manner: 'Well, you expect us to have sympathy with you. But you don't seem to understand that East Germany is being depopulated, while here in West Germany we have to cope with an overflow of people.'

Elisabeth thought he was sizing all four of them up while speaking. But then he swiftly handed the papers back to Ludwig, saying, 'OK' and moved on to the next person.

Elisabeth gazed at Ludwig and gave a sigh of relief. It meant they could stay.

While waiting for the rest of the people to be dealt with, she looked behind her and noticed the Russian border checkpoint – a mere 100 metres away. A large iron gate with an oversized portrait of Stalin on top was flanked by huge red flags. On either side stood a Russian guard staring in their direction. The picture of a triumphal arch came to Elisabeth's mind. She was flabbergasted. What was happening to her country?

In the end, all the people were allowed to stay. Elisabeth saw the officer step aside with his aides. Presumably they were discussing how to proceed. She heard the word 'tractor' mentioned. Where were they taking them from here, she wondered?

After only a few moments the officer came back and announced: 'You will be driven to our camp for the night. But there is only space for women and children on the vehicle. All men have to walk. My colleague here will give you directions.'

So the men were ordered to one side and soon started on their walk. When Anja saw her father walk off she became extremely anxious: 'Are they taking Daddy away?' she cried out, sobbing bitterly.

'No, darling,' Elisabeth put her arm around her and tried to calm her down: 'He has to walk with the other men. He'll be with us at the camp.' She could see her little girl's distress and she was grateful to have Friedrich with her to help explain to Anja what was happening.

Luckily, a lorry arrived before long. The women and children were helped on to it, while their luggage was taken separately, on a small van. They were sitting on low benches. Elisabeth held Anja close by her side, wiping her tears from her face, reassuring her that she would see her daddy very soon. Friedrich was at the very back of the lorry. Elisabeth was touched when she noticed that a soldier had put his arm around him to keep him from falling off. He looked so friendly. She heard him ask: 'Are you all right?' Friedrich nodded and smiled at him. A British soldier protecting a German boy! Half a year ago they might have been fighting each other.

After a ten minute drive over rather uneven ground they arrived at the camp. Together with a crowd of other refugees they were shown into a wooden hut. On either side stood long rows of bunk beds. They looked clean, and Elisabeth was happy to see that there was an extra blanket for each bed. Although it was only the early part of October, it felt quite chilly, and she couldn't see any heaters.

While they were putting their cases and rucksacks into shelves beside their beds, a nurse came in. She rang a little bell to get everyone's attention, and said with a smile: 'The evening meal will be served in the main block in half an hour. I'm sure you're all hungry.'

'Oh yes, we are,' a little woman next to Elisabeth said quietly. 'I wonder what's on the menu?' Elisabeth smiled at her. Whatever it was she would be grateful for it.

'There's one other thing I have to tell you,' the nurse continued, 'you are required to report to Block A later, to be de-loused.'

People looked up in surprise. Some were giggling, others seemed appalled at the prospect. Elisabeth was quite amused. Obviously it was necessary with so many dirty people passing through the camp.

Friedrich asked: 'What is de-lousing?'

Elisabeth said: 'Oh, it's nothing to worry about. The nurse has a big syringe and sprays your arms and legs with a white powder. That helps us not to attract lice. I had to do it once when I was a nurse in Glogau.'

'Is Daddy coming soon?' Anja asked, getting very agitated.

'Yes, sweetheart, I'm sure he'll be here in a minute. Why don't you go and stand at the door over there. Then you see him when he comes.' Turning to Friedrich she said: 'You go, too. I can get our beds ready in the meantime.'

She was thinking of Ludwig on his march. How long would it take the men to get here? Hopefully they would be here in time for their evening meal.

But she didn't have to wait long. Suddenly she heard Anja calling at the top of her voice: 'Daddy!' In an instant she had run out towards him and now led him into the hut.

'There you are.' Elisabeth heaved a sigh of relief. 'Did you get on all right?' She could see how tired he looked.

'It was quite a march. I'm happy I'm here now.' He took them all in his arms and said to Elisabeth: 'I promised you we'd make it, didn't I?'

'Yes, you did, and you've kept your word,' she answered, feeling tears of exhaustion rising up in her eyes. What a day it had been. She could hardly believe that they were now in free West Germany.

'Are we going to eat now?' Anja was getting impatient when she saw other people walking out of the hut. 'I'm so hungry.'

'Of course, Anja, we're all hungry.' Elisabeth said in a firm tone. 'Just wait until Daddy has had a little rest. Then we'll all go together.'

In the main block, they had to queue up for their food. They sat on benches at long wooden tables. Elisabeth was very pleased about the nutritious meal they were given: a tasty vegetable soup with a big pair of Frankfurters and a thick slice of bread, followed by caramel blancmange. Ludwig even got a second helping.

When they had finished their meal, Elisabeth informed Ludwig, with a twinkle in her eye: 'And now we have to go and be de-loused.'

'What?' Ludwig sounded astonished.

'Yes, it's a requirement here,' Elisabeth explained, 'we were told about it earlier.'

There was more queuing at Block A, but it all went well. The children took it in good spirits and before they knew it they were fast asleep, back in their bunks.

Ludwig and Elisabeth sat up and talked for a short while, before they too, lay down to sleep. Elisabeth was reminded of the night back in February, when she and the children had spent the night in similar circumstances in a hotel room in Halle, while Dresden was burning. But of course, it was different now. She had Ludwig with her again. Would they sleep in proper beds tomorrow night?

31

Arriving in Eschwege

The next morning, Elisabeth was woken by some of her fellow refugees who were moving about in the room quietly. It was still dark.

'You're up early,' she whispered to a woman standing next to her bed.

'Yes, we want to get away as soon as possible,' the woman replied.

'Where are you going?'

'To Cologne, to stay with my sister. It's a long way off. They say the trains are not very good. And it may take a long while before they let us out of here.'

'Why is that?' Elisabeth was puzzled.

'Well, don't you know, there are hundreds of people in this camp. It'll take ages to check everyone. I have our papers, so we should be OK.'

With that the woman and her husband disappeared.

Elisabeth felt quite dazed. She saw that Ludwig and the children were still sleeping soundly. Should she wake them up? She wasn't sure how far they were from their destination, Eschwege. They, too, would probably have to travel a long time.

But she wasn't going to worry. She lay back on her mattress, trying to relax. Closing her eyes, the memories of the previous day came flooding into her mind – the walk through the park, hiding in the bushes, wading through the stream, and most frightening of all, seeing

Anja standing beside the Russian soldier. Then the interrogation at the check point. She could hardly believe that they had made it. They had crossed the border. They were in West Germany. Even in these strange surroundings of the refugee camp she felt safe.

Suddenly she heard Anja's voice: 'Mummy, wake up. It's morning.'

She must have drifted off again. 'Oh, Anja, darling. Did you sleep well?'

'Yes, I did. I dreamt we were in a train, and I saw soldiers outside on the platform. They had rifles, but they didn't shoot at us.'

Elisabeth was taken aback by Anja's words. It suddenly came home to her what a dreadful experience yesterday's event must have been for Anja as well as for Friedrich. Would it have damaged them psychologically? She had been unable to shield them from what they had gone through. So far they had shown remarkable resilience and she hoped that in time they would forget about it all.

'Let's get ready now. We have a long journey in front of us,' she heard Ludwig's authoritative voice.

Quickly they packed their cases and rucksacks and soon found themselves queuing for breakfast in the main block. Elisabeth was happy to see there was porridge, and also bread and jam, and tea. That was going to give them a good start to their day.

She was amazed at how well things were organized in this camp. Where were all these people heading, she wondered? The officer at the checkpoint was right: West Germany was overflowing with new residents. Would he have to interrogate a new lot of refugees today?

She was grateful that on their way out they were each handed a small packet of sandwiches wrapped in brown paper. It would see them through the next hours at least.

Then there was more queuing to be endured. As the woman had told her earlier in the morning, the procedure of checking people's documents seemed to take forever. She saw that many refugees stayed behind. What would happen to them?

At last they were allowed to go. They walked to the main gate of the camp, where they waited to be transported to Schöningen. Elisabeth noticed that the vehicle was the same lorry that had brought her and the children to the camp the night before.

At Schöningen station Ludwig immediately went to buy the tickets.

'Our train leaves in five minutes, from platform 5 ,' he called out. They ran as fast as they could. No sooner had they climbed into the train, with an official pushing their luggage in for them, than it started moving.

'That was lucky,' Elisabeth sat back in her seat, heaving a sigh of relief and smiling at her family.

'Yes,' Ludwig said, 'if it goes on like this, we should make it to Eschwege tonight.

'Is it very far to Eschwege?' Elisabeth could hear a wearisome tone in Anja's voice and she just wished that their travels wouldn't last much longer.

'Let's hope the trains run on time' Ludwig said in a calming voice, 'then it won't take too long. But you have to be patient.'

'At least we won't have to wade through a stream again,' Friedrich remarked.

'No, certainly not. That's all behind us now.' Ludwig answered, stroking his arm gently.

'Is Eschwege a nice town, like Quedlinburg?' Anja asked.

'Yes, I'm sure you'll like it there,' her father replied, and Elisabeth could hear strong conviction in his voice. He wasn't going to let them down.

After about an hour and a half they reached Braunschweig, where they had to change trains. By now, Elisabeth was used to it, but here it was very different. She wasn't prepared for what she encountered. There was no proper platform to step out on, instead there was only gravel. When she looked up, she could see a huge ruin in front of her.

She looked at Ludwig, gasping: 'Is that the station?'

'Yes,' he answered, 'or rather: it was. The centre of Braunschweig was completely destroyed in a bombing raid last year.'

Elisabeth shook her head in horror. She had only ever seen pictures of ruins like this.

While they were looking around for their next train, they heard an announcement over a loudspeaker: 'Passengers for the following destinations, please walk along the path, signposted: "To the trains" for your connections'.

Ludwig listened intently: 'Göttingen – that's us,' he said. 'Come, let's follow the sign.'

Braunschweig- ruins

As they started walking, Elisabeth realized that large sections of the rail tracks were missing. The dust path led them first across a wide overgrown area. On either side big heaps of rubble were showing through the rough grass. Surely, this had once been the road, Elisabeth thought. Now they were approaching a gutted church. Its damaged tower, rising high up into the sky, resembled a hollow tooth. Opposite stood the remains of a house, with gaping windows. There were large black patches on the walls, a certain indication that fire had swept through it. Would people have had the chance to flee to their air raid shelters before the bombs fell on their houses? How many may have died in these ruins? Elisabeth was aghast at what she saw. This, the centre of a big town, had turned into a ghost city.

She was glad that Ludwig was hurrying them on. She didn't like the children to be exposed to this sight for long. Friedrich, especially would certainly never forget it.

After about ten minutes the path led back to the rail tracks, and soon they came to a small station. When Ludwig enquired about their connection to Göttingen, he was told that they would have to wait for over an hour.

Elisabeth turned to him in dismay: 'Where shall we go? There doesn't seem to be a waiting room here.'

'No,' he said. She could hear weariness in his voice now. 'Perhaps we can find somewhere to sit outside.'

'There's a little park over there,' Friedrich pointed across the road.

'Oh, Friedrich, well spotted, let's go there.' Ludwig strode across and they followed.

'We can have our sandwiches here,' Elisabeth suggested, when they had found a little dry spot on the grass to sit down.

While they were resting, Elisabeth watched several men in suits standing in front of a ruined building opposite, seemingly discussing the reconstruction of it. One was pointing to various parts of the house, another one made notes. A photographer had put up his tripod and was about to take a picture of the building. After a while the men walked on, presumably to inspect another ruin. How long would it take to rebuild this whole city, she wondered?

The children were getting restless and Elisabeth encouraged them to wander about a little bit.

Eventually, it was time to go back to the station, and soon they were on the move again. It was getting dark when they arrived in Göttingen. To their disappointment, the station was being closed for the night, just as they got off the train.

When Ludwig told the station master where they were heading, Elisabeth heard him say: 'The next train to Eschwege leaves at 5.30 in the morning.'

She thought the man probably guessed they were refugees. He looked at them with pity in his eyes and said: 'There's a school nearby that has been converted into a camp. You'll find a bed there for the night, I'm sure. Go along Station Road here. Then turn into the second street on the right. There it is.'

'Thank you,' Ludwig said. 'That's very kind of you.'

At the school, Red Cross helpers gave them a warm welcome, offering them hot soup and slices of bread with cheese and an apple each. As they would have to leave early, before breakfast, one helper kindly handed Elisabeth a packet of sandwiches for their journey. Tired and weary, they quickly went to lie down on their bunk beds in a classroom. It would be a very short night.

Eschwege – on river Werra

Elisabeth was the first to wake in the morning. She felt very excited. It was Saturday, 13 October. This was to be the last day of their travels. They were heading towards their final destination: Eschwege. Ludwig had told her a little about this town on the river Werra, in the county of Hesse. It sounded delightful. He said it had escaped the bombing entirely. She was looking forward to seeing it.

She woke her family, and soon they were ready to go off to the station. It was still dark. There was the old station master, waving them goodbye. The train was on time, and for once they were by themselves in a compartment. She was surprised how fast this train was moving. Hopefully the journey wouldn't take very long.

'Is Opa coming to the station, when we arrive?' Anja asked, looking expectantly at her father.

'Oh no, darling, he doesn't know we're on our way now.'

'Does he live far from the station?' Friedrich wanted to know.

Elisabeth sensed that both her children were getting excited at the prospect of arriving in their new home town soon.

'Well, it's a fair walk. It'll probably take us half an hour with our luggage.'

'Is Eschwege very hilly?' Friedrich's interest in the town was obviously growing.

'Not very hilly, no,' Ludwig answered, 'but there is a lovely hill nearby, called "Leuchtberg" with a tower on top. You can see it from wherever you are in the town.'

Elisabeth could see Anja's mind working, as she asked: 'Is it like the castle in Quedlinburg?'

189

'It's not a castle, just a tall tower. But there is a castle in the town, as well. I'll show you everything when we go for walks together.'

When Elisabeth heard Anja mention Quedlinburg, she couldn't help thinking of her parents. They would be wondering how the family's travels had gone. Would they be able to follow them here one day soon? She must write to them straight away.

In the first light of the morning, she could make out gentle hills in the distance, and it wasn't long before she saw the first rays of the rising sun. It was going to be a fine day. A good omen!

After two hours the train pulled into Eschwege station. They had arrived. Slowly they walked along the platform and out of the station building. The air was mild and clear, and the trees on the wide green in front of them showed off their beautiful autumn colours. Elisabeth could sense what a lovely town this was.

She watched the children as they kept pointing to particular places.

Eschwege – Dietemann tower

'Look at that a little tower up there.' Anja had spotted the top of the castle building.

'That's the Dietemann tower.' Ludwig explained. 'In the old times the little man used to come out every hour and blow his horn. You'll learn all about that at school, I'm sure.'

Eschwege – half timbered house

'The half-timbered houses are similar to the ones in Quedlinburg,' Friedrich said. Elisabeth admired his sharp observation.

'Yes, you're right,' Ludwig replied, 'they were probably built at the same time, in the seventeenth century.'

While they were stopping for a while, resting from carrying their cases, Ludwig suddenly pointed his finger in a certain direction: 'Can you see that church spire in the distance?'

They all gazed to where he was pointing.

'Yes, I can,' Anja had spotted it quickly.

'Well, that's where we have to aim for. Opposite the church is Opa's house.'

'Let's run,' both children shouted at once. Nothing seemed to be holding them back now.

'Not so fast, please,' Elisabeth tried to keep them in check. 'We're far too early, anyway. Opa might not be up yet.'

'Oh yes, he'll be up. He's an old soldier,' Ludwig laughed. 'And if not, we'll have to wake him up, won't we?'

With that they took their cases and walked as fast as they could. When they got near to the church, they heard the clock strike. Elisabeth counted: it was 8 o'clock. Ludwig beckoned to them to cross the road, and then stopped in front of a lovely half-timbered house.

'Here we are,' he said, putting his case down. He rang the bell.

They waited, full of anticipation. Elisabeth remembered that day in January when she had said goodbye to her father-in-law in Glogau. How many miles had they all travelled since then? Now she heard footsteps on a staircase inside. The door flung open, and there was Opa Giertz.

'Hello,' he cried out, 'you are here. Do come in.'

Elisabeth thought he looked as youthful as ever.

'Opa, Opa!' The children flew into his outstretched arms. He held them and kissed them both, and then he embraced Ludwig and Elisabeth.

'It's wonderful to see you,' he said, with a huge smile on his face. 'Let me help you with your cases.'

Energetically, he took the biggest case and led the way upstairs.

As she walked in, Elisabeth was quite overcome with emotion. Their odyssey was at an end. They were free. What would the future hold?

32

New Beginnings

It was the late afternoon of Christmas Eve 1945. Elisabeth sat down on one of the three wooden chairs in their small family room – exhausted but happy. She felt that a small miracle had happened. There, in front of her, on the oblong table, which served in turn as dining table, writing desk and worktop for all household chores, stood a little Christmas tree.

It was sparsely decorated with some strips of tinsel, a few baubles made from balls of wool, two rugged wooden figures, a paper angel and just three white candles, one of which was already half burnt down. At the top of the tree was a little straw star that Friedrich had made at school.

Until two days ago, Elisabeth had been resigned to the fact that they wouldn't have a Christmas tree this year. She had looked everywhere in the weekly market and in greengrocers' shops, but there didn't seem to be any trees. She had told her children that they would have to be content without one. Friedrich, in particular, was very sad and became almost withdrawn during the days before Christmas. It meant such a lot to him. No doubt he remembered the beautiful big tree of last year in their old home.

But then, the day before yesterday, her neighbour, Miss Peters, in whom she had confided, told her of a family in a nearby street who would let her have a little tree for a small sum of money. They had connections to a forestry commission and were willing to help out.

Elisabeth and Ludwig had rushed over in the early evening and brought the tree home, hiding it in the cellar, in order to surprise the children on Christmas Eve.

To give her time to decorate the tree, Ludwig had taken the children out this afternoon, first to visit their grandfather. What a blessing that he had found a good home in an old people's residence soon after they arrived in Eschwege in October. He was now 81 years old and Elisabeth was relieved to know that he was well looked after in a comfortable place.

After their visit, Ludwig and the children would go on to attend the Christmas Eve family service at their church. So Elisabeth had enough time to get the little room prepared for their evening's celebrations. In addition to the straw star, Friedrich had made paper chains. How diligent he had been colouring paper sheets with water paints and then cutting narrow strips and forming them into little rings. He had been so patient when they wouldn't immediately stick together. At school he had learnt how to make glue from flour. He was so proud of his chains, which certainly brightened up the grey walls of this small room and also looked effective on the greenery Elisabeth had arranged in an old vase her neighbour had kindly lent her.

She gave a sigh when she looked at the scantily wrapped gifts she had placed under the tree. In front of the little packets sat four gingerbread men the baker had given her this morning. They looked quite forlorn and were a poor replacement for the traditional 'Christmas plate' each member of the family would usually have, heaped with special biscuits, chocolates, nuts, apples and oranges.

Sitting there by herself, she couldn't help thinking of their Christmas a year ago. How delighted she had been to find the beautiful doll Brigitte for Anja. Friedrich had been so good letting her have his train set in exchange for the doll. She thought of all the other lovely presents she had been able to give the children. And now?

But she knew it was wrong to dwell on the past, as so many of her fellow refugees seemed to do. There was no going back. Her homeland Silesia, was now in Polish hands. Her home town Glogau lay in ruins, after several Russian air raids. It would be the task of young Poles to rebuild it and make it their home in future.

Here, she had to look forward for her children's sake, and be strong for them. It hadn't been easy settling in over the last three months, but she had experienced a lot of kindness from strangers and felt her family had found an adequate first new home in this pleasant town which had escaped the bombing entirely.

School had started soon after their arrival in October. Friedrich had got a place in the local grammar school, and Anja was happy at her new primary school. Already, they had made good friends, especially among other refugee children, and despite their frequent complaints of being hungry, they were remarkably well. Ludwig was still looking for a proper work place as a journalist, but in the meantime was making some money in a factory producing knitting wool.

Although they were poor now, having lost their home, they were together as a family – and for that she would for ever be grateful. Surely, there would be a good and happy future for them in this place.

She picked up her mother's Christmas letter, which had arrived a couple of days ago. How happy she was to read that her parents had been invited to spend Christmas Eve and Christmas Day with the Kuhrau family. These lovely friends had surely kept their promise to look after the old people for her. Nevertheless, Elisabeth hoped they might be able to join them here in Eschwege in the not too distant future.

There was a Christmas card from Gerda, too. She seemd very happy writing about baby Ruth, who was growing fast, crawling all over the place and keeping the family amused with her babble.

Getting up from her hard chair to draw the curtains, Elisabeth looked at the little tree again and felt like shouting out in triumph. She would take it as a symbol of a new beginning.